HOUGHTON MIFFLIN

My Math Activity Book

Level
K

HOUGHTON MIFFLIN

Boston • Atlanta • Dallas • Geneva, Illinois • Palo Alto • Princeton

ISBN: 0-395-87648-6

6789-PO-03 02 01 00 99 98

CONTENTS

Name _____

 green

 brown

Children color the frogs green. Then they color the monkeys brown.

August/September: Use when children are familiar with the *Counting Tape*.

I

Children color one pair of matching boots red. Then they color another pair blue and the other pair yellow.

Name _____

  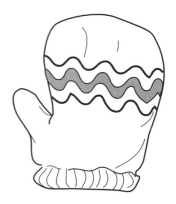

 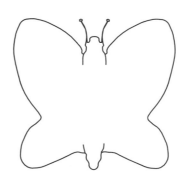 

Turtle: Children color the apple red. Then they color the object **before** the apple brown. **Frog:** Children color the object **between** the ship and the kite purple. **Fish:** Children color the flower yellow. Then they color the object **after** the flower green.

August/September: Use when children are familiar with the *Counting Tape.*

Same Position

Discuss with children whether each book comes **before, between,** or **after.** Then children color the pictures of the books that are in the same position as the book in the first picture in each row.

August/September: Use when children are familiar with the *Counting Tape.*

Name _____

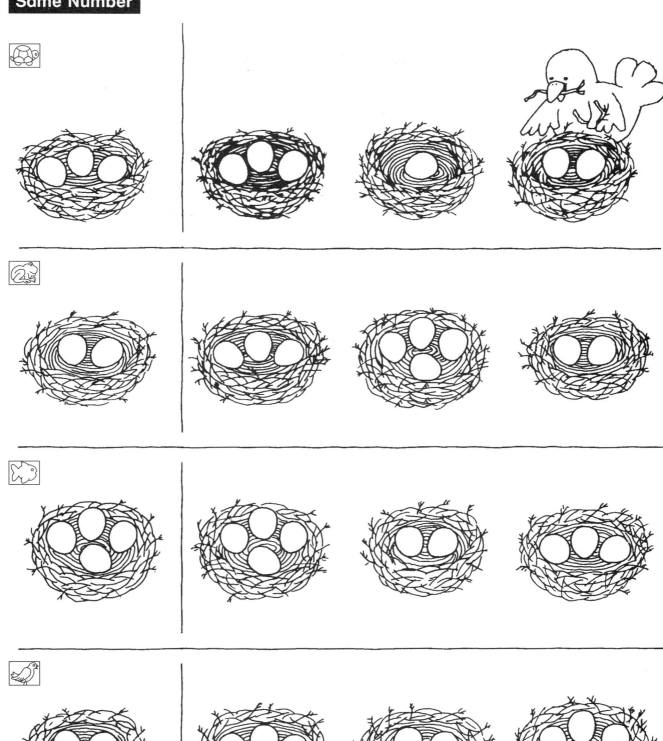

Children circle the nest that has the same number of eggs as the nest in the first picture in each row.

August/September: Use when children are familiar with the *Clip Collection*.

Sort the Shapes

Children color the two fish that are the same.

Sort the Blocks

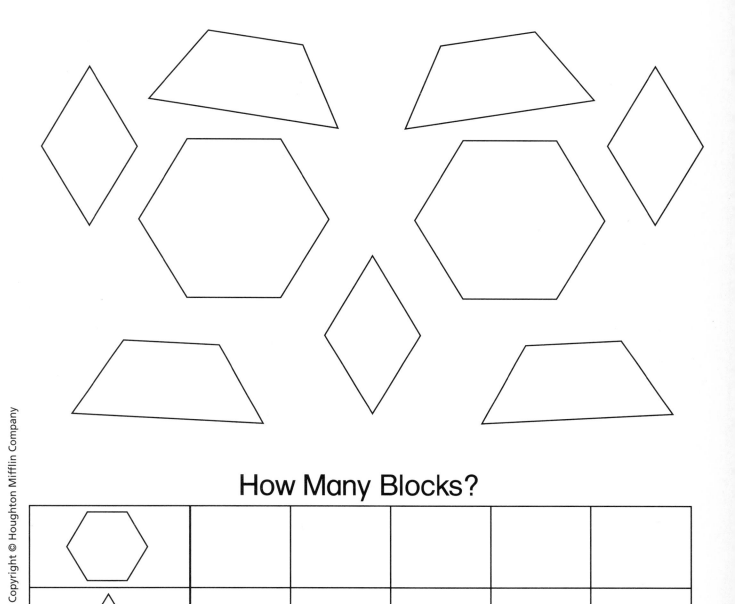

How Many Blocks?

Children cover the shapes with pattern blocks. Then they sort the blocks by shape and color one box in the graph for each corresponding block.

August/September: Use when children are familiar with the *Graph.*

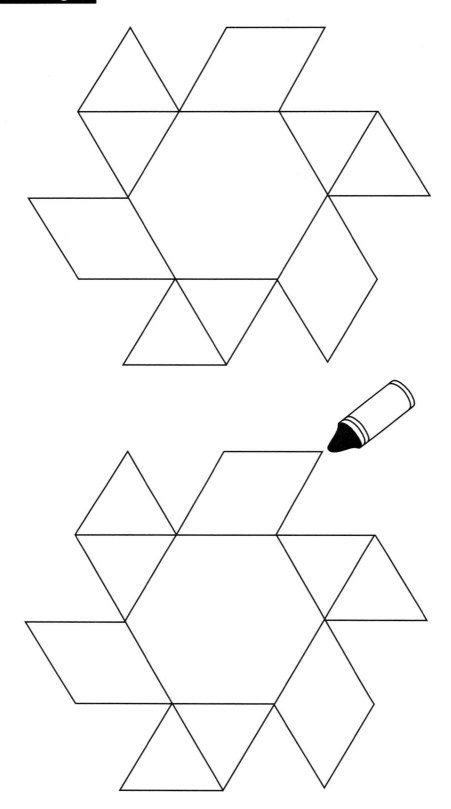

Children place corresponding pattern blocks on the top design and then color the bottom design to match.

Name _____

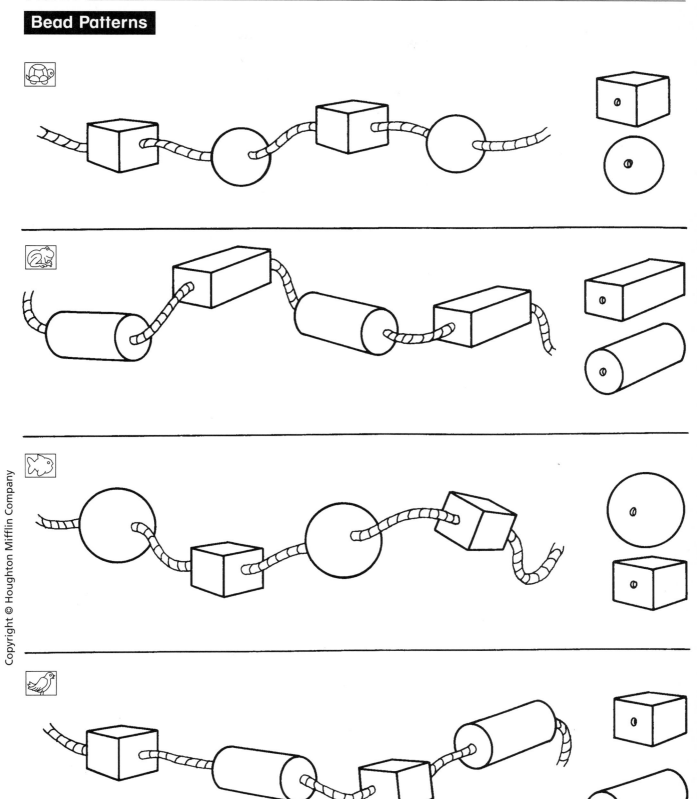

Together, name the beads in order and then have children circle the bead that comes next in each row.

August/September: Use when children are familiar with *Connecting Cubes*.

9

Animal Patterns

Together, name the animals in order and then have children circle the animal that comes next in each row.

Name _____

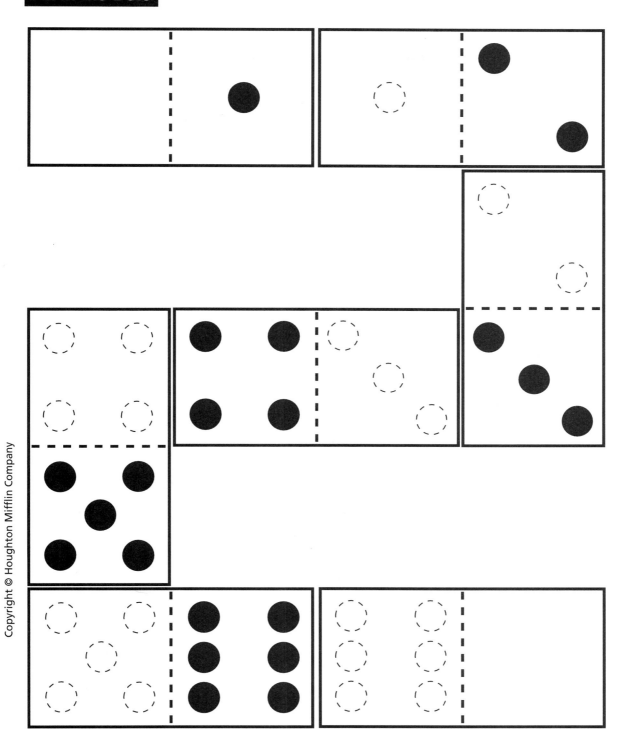

Children color the dots on the dominoes. When completed, ask children to name each domino half and point to its matching domino half.

August/September: Use when children are familiar with *Dominoes.*

Sort the Objects

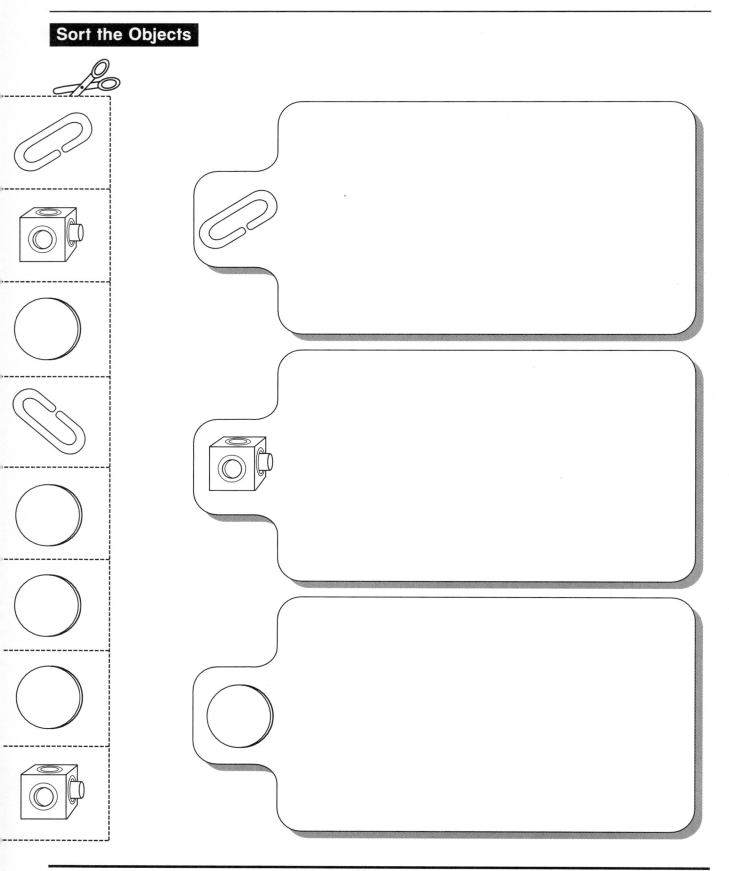

Children cut out the objects, sort them, and then paste them in the appropriate space.

Name _____

Turtle: Children draw lines to match each hat to a head. **Frog:** Children draw a hat on each head.

August/September: Use when children are familiar with *Literature Corner*.

How Many Blocks?

Turtle: Children color the object **after** the flower blue; the object **before** the flower orange. **Frog:** Children place corresponding pattern blocks on the top design. Children color the bottom design to match. **Fish:** Children then sort and graph the pattern blocks.

Name _____

How Many Presents?

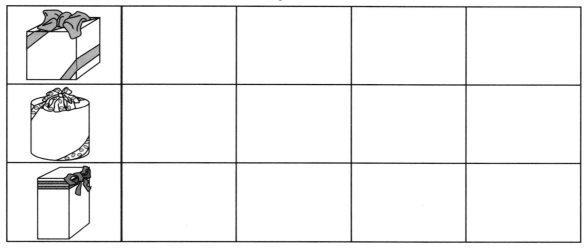

Children color the appropriate box in the graph for each present. You may want children to cross out the presents in the basket as they record them on the graph.

October: Use when children are familiar with the *Graph.*

15

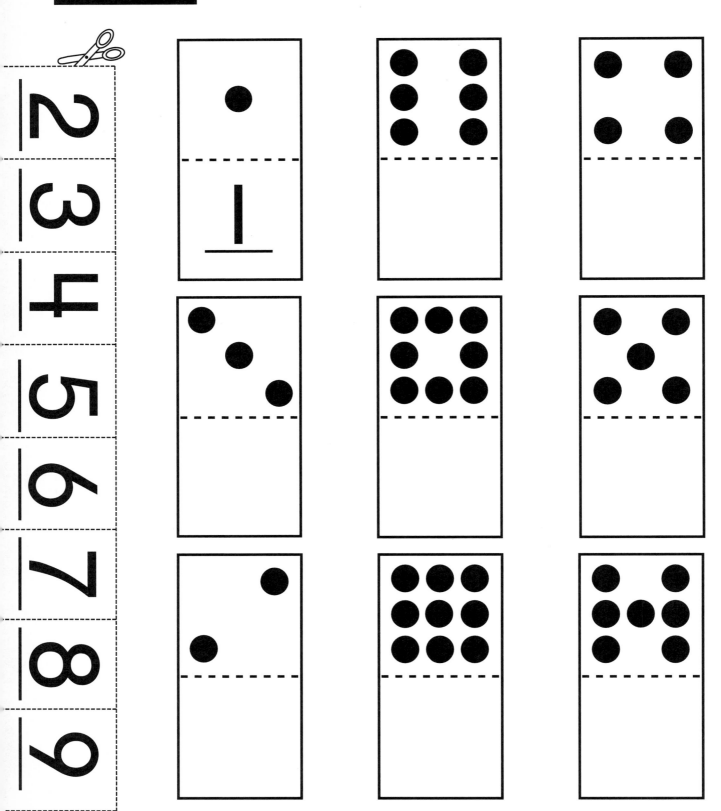

Children cut out digit cards and paste each one under the dots on the domino that shows that number.

Name _____

Children color the object or animal in each picture that is **above.**

October: Use when children are familiar with *What Is It?*

Which Is Below?

Children mark an X on the object or animal in each picture that is **below**.

Name _____

Pattern Trains

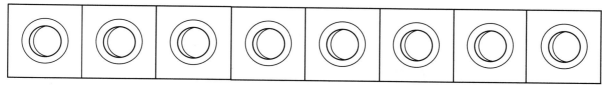

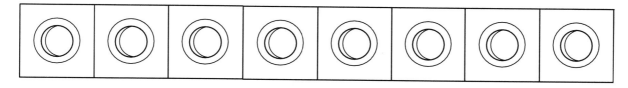

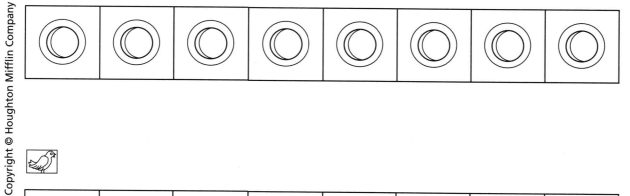

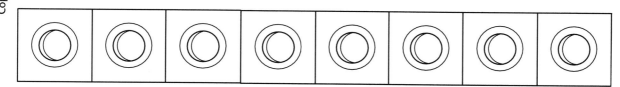

Turtle: Children use two different colors of connecting cubes on top of the train to make an AAAB pattern.
Frog: Children color the squares to represent the cubes used in the Turtle row. **Fish and Bird:** Children repeat the steps above using two different colors of cubes.

October: Use when children are familiar with *Copying and Extending a Pattern Train.*   **1 9**

October: Use when children are familiar with *Quick As You Can.*   **2 1**

Groups to 5

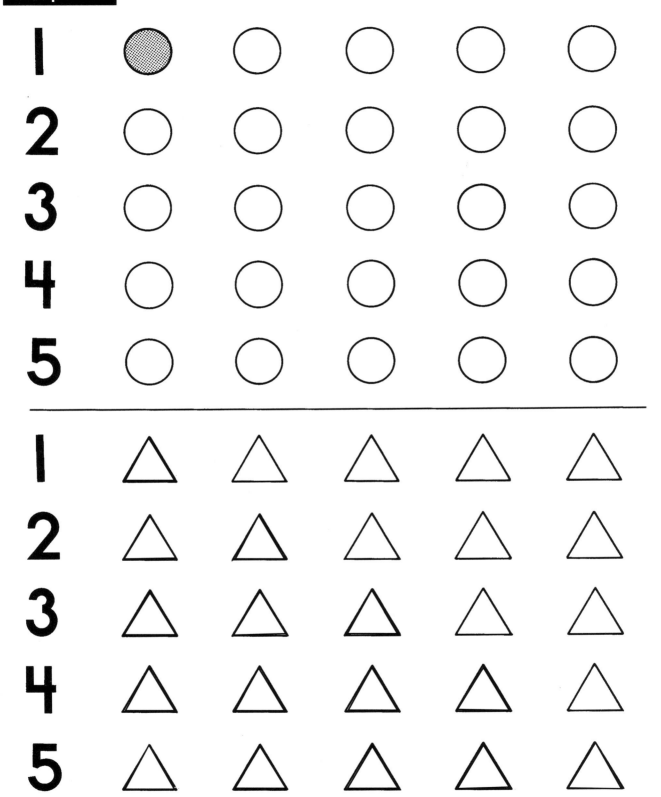

Children color as many objects in each row as indicated by the number at the beginning of the row.

Name _____

Children color as many spots on each dog as indicated by the number on the dog's tag.

October: Use when children are familiar with *Quick As You Can.*

One-to-One Match

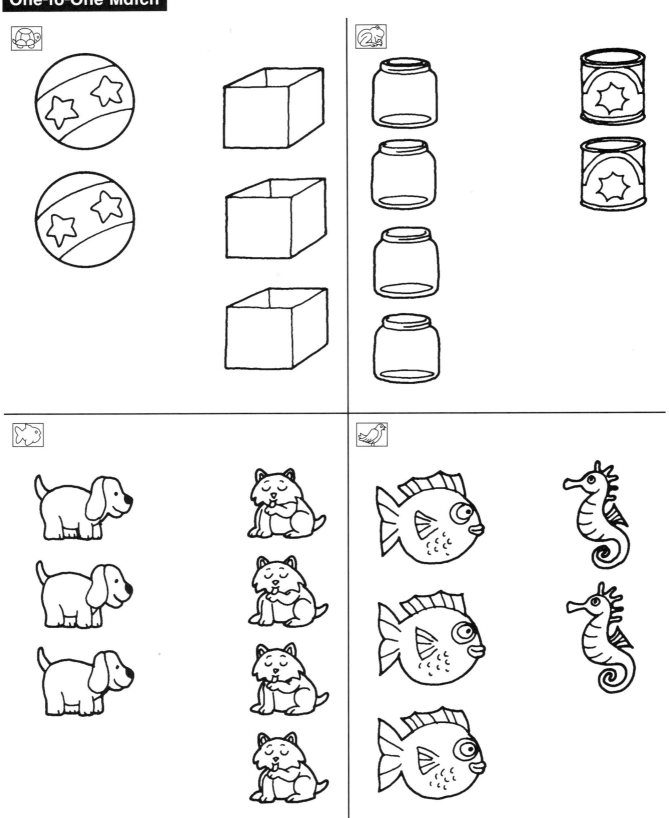

In each box, children draw lines to match the objects or animals. Then they circle the group that has more.

Name _____

Children color the object or animal that is on the **left** in each picture.

October: Use when children are familiar with *Left-Right Tug.*

left    right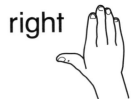

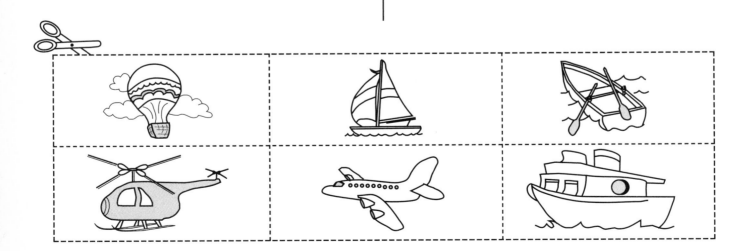

Have children identify the cutouts. Children cut and paste vehicles that go in the water on the left and vehicles that go in the air on the right.

Name _____

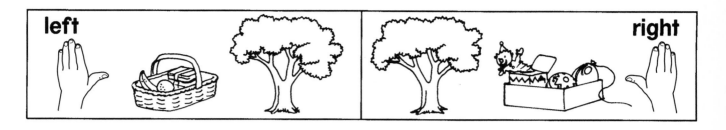

left   right

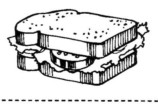

Have children identify the cutouts. Children cut and paste pictures of food on the left side of the tree and pictures of toys on the right side of the tree.

October: Use when children are familiar with *Left-Right Tug.*

Name _____

Which Is the Same?

  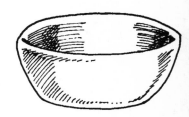

 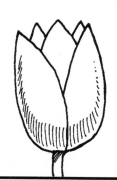 

Children color the pictures that are the same in each row.

October: Use when children are familiar with *Classroom Project*.

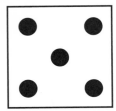 4 6 5

 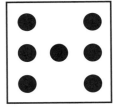 7 8 6

 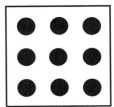 8 9 7

  6 5 7

  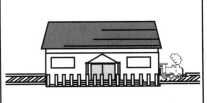 

Turtle, Frog, Fish, and Bird: Children circle the number represented by the domino in each row.
Squirrel: Children color the left train blue and the right train red.

Writing 0–5

Children trace the two numbers at the beginning of each row and then write the number three more times.

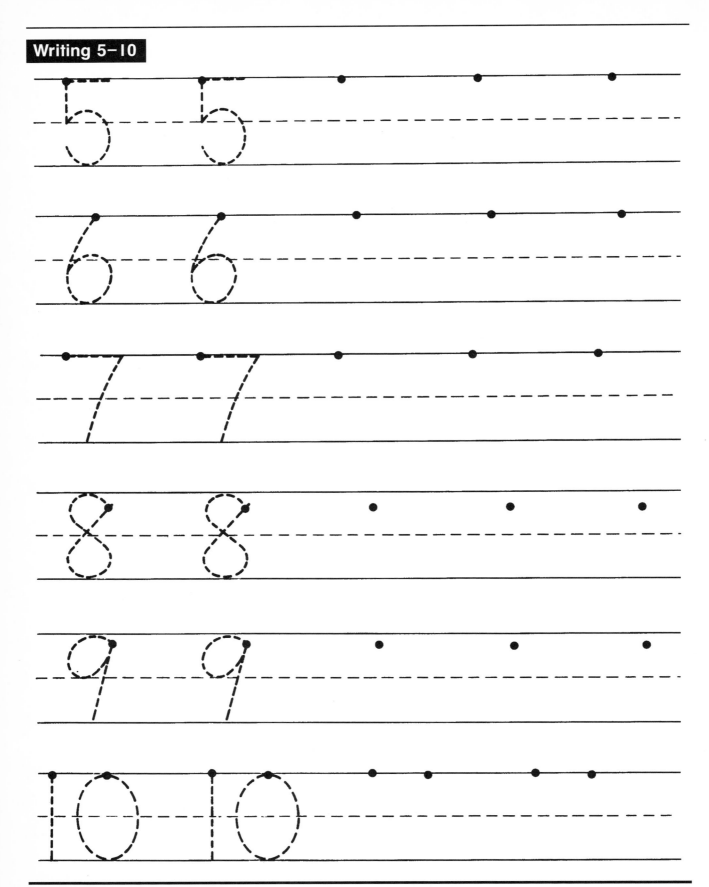

Children trace the two numbers at the beginning of each row and then write the number.

Name _____

Count the Cubes

9
8
7
6
5
4
3
2
1

Children cut out numerals and paste them beside the corresponding cube towers.

November: Use when children are familiar with *Match My Stack*.

Name _____

Odd and Even

2	4	6	8	10
12	14	16	18	20
22	24	26	28	30
32	34	36	38	40
42	44	46	48	50

1	2	3	4	5	6	7	8	9	10
11	12	13	14	15	16	17	18	19	20
21	22	23	24	25	26	27	28	29	30
31	32	33	34	35	36	37	38	39	40
41	42	43	44	45	46	47	48	49	50

Turtle: Children use the numbers to skip-count by 2. **Frog:** Children color the even numbers blue. Then they color the odd numbers red.

November: Use during the third week of the month with the *Calendar*.

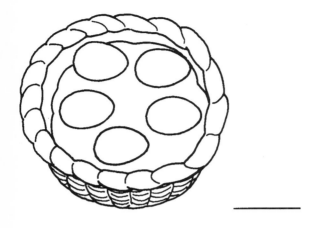

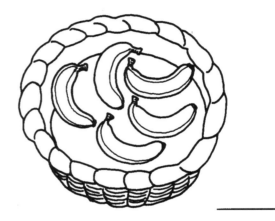

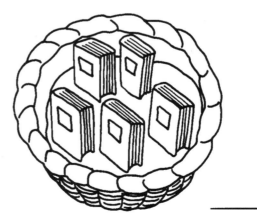

Children circle the pictures that show 5. Then they write the numeral 5 next to each picture that shows 5 objects or animals.

Name _____

Which Is Shorter?

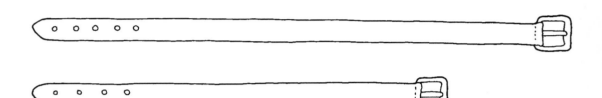

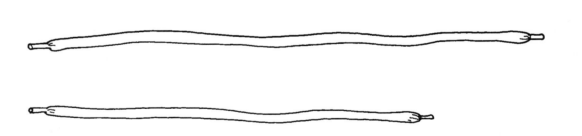

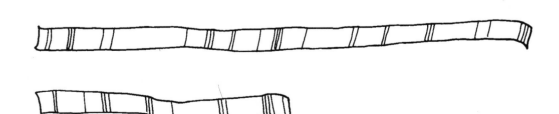

In each section, children color the **shorter** item.

November: Use when children are familiar with *Length Comparing.*

Long or Short?

In each section, children circle the **shortest** item and put an X on the **longest** item.

Name _____

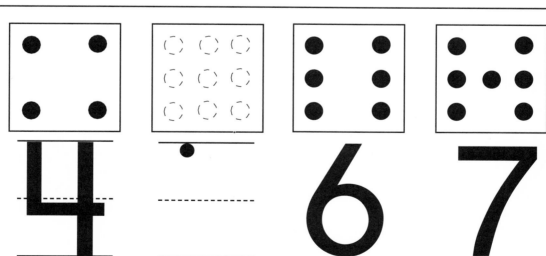

What Is Missing?

Using the domino icons as models, children shade in the correct number and placement of dots in each unshaded domino and then write the numeral.

November: Use when children are familiar with *Counting Tape to Ten*.

How Many Sides?

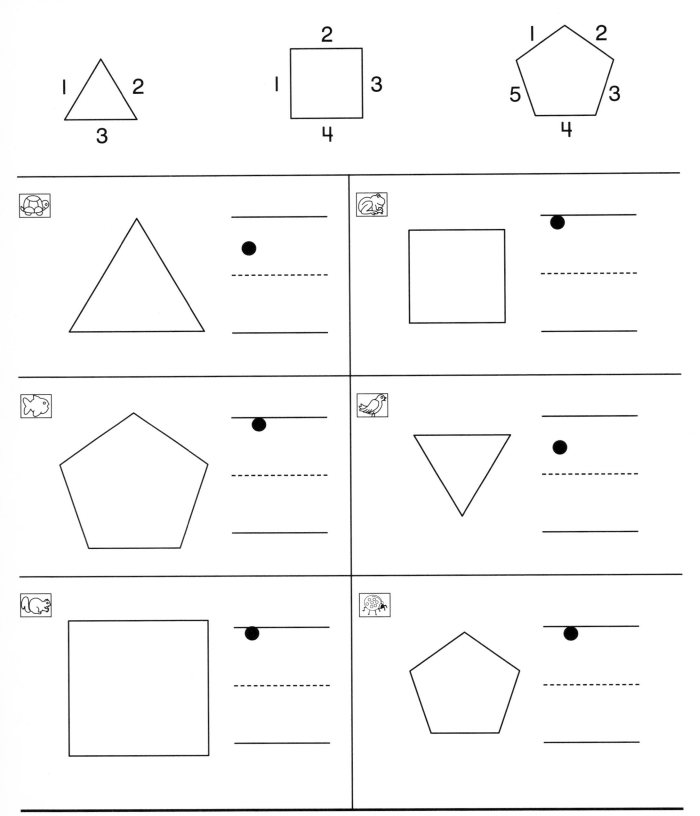

In each row, children state the number of sides for each shape and then record that numeral next to the shape.

Name _____

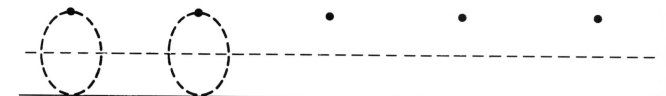

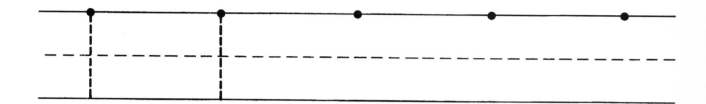

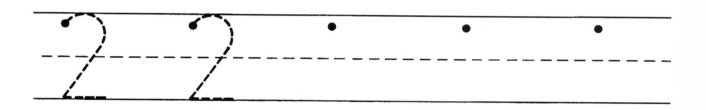

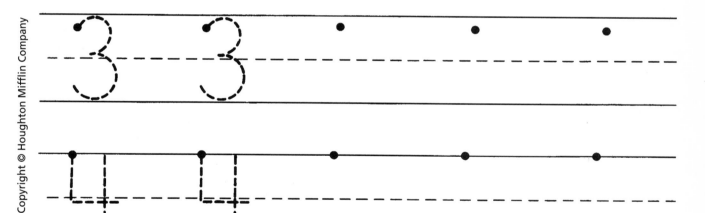

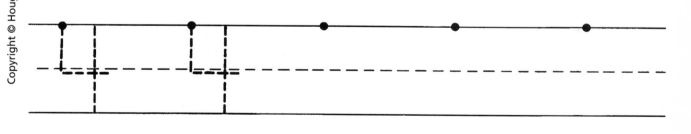

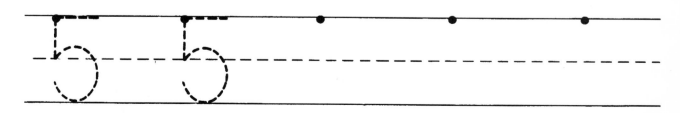

Copyright © Houghton Mifflin Company

Children trace the two numbers at the beginning of each row and then write the number three more times.

November: Use when children are familiar with *Days in School Game*.

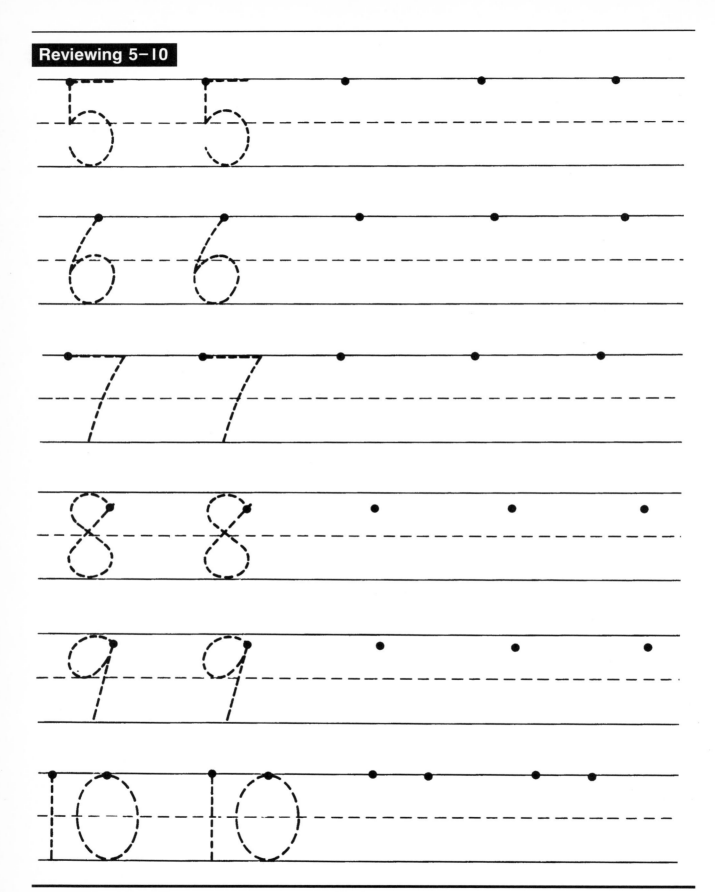

Children trace the two numbers at the beginning of each row and then write the number.

Name _____

Count the Dots

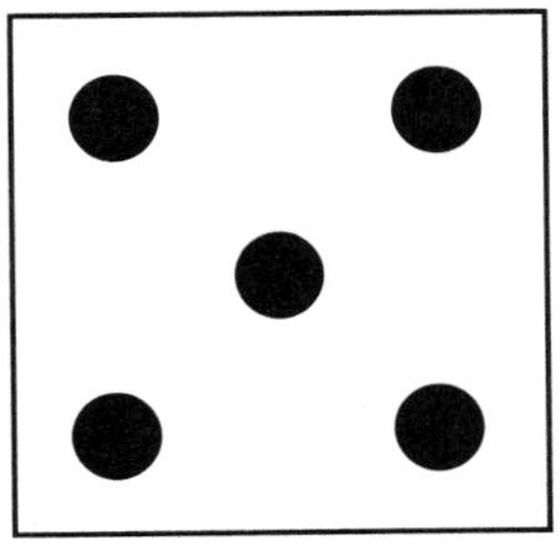

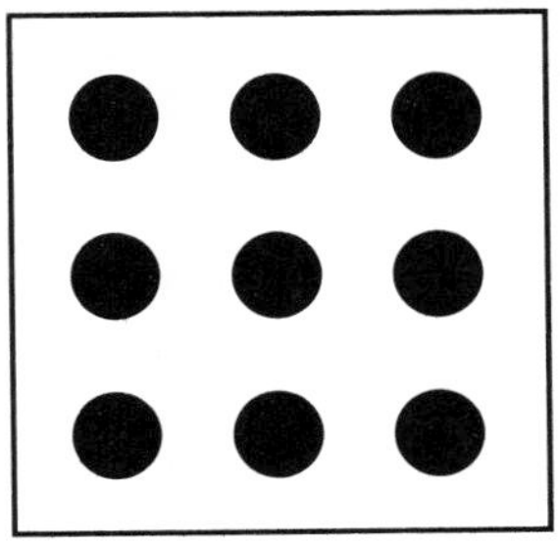

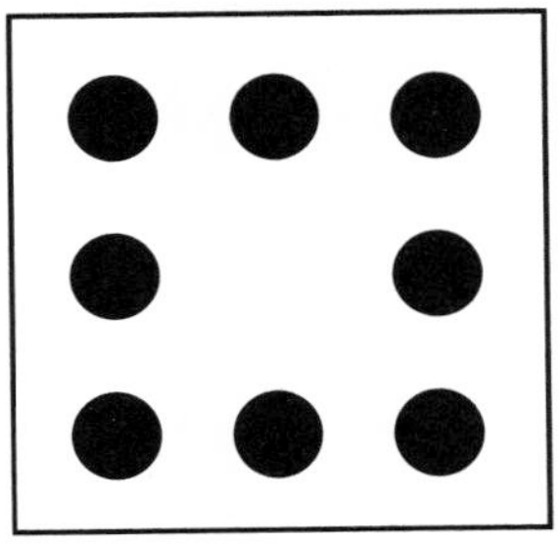

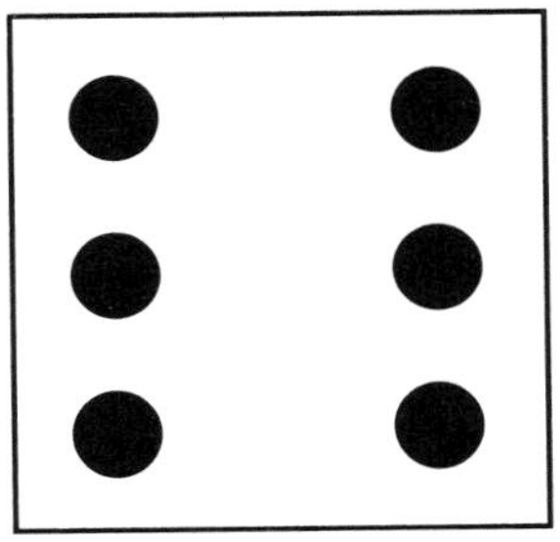

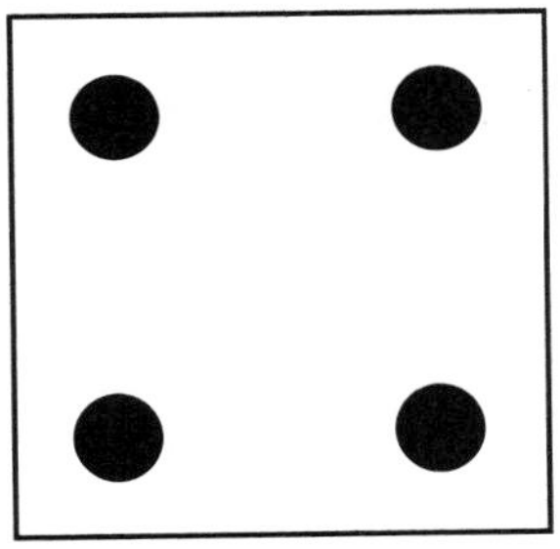

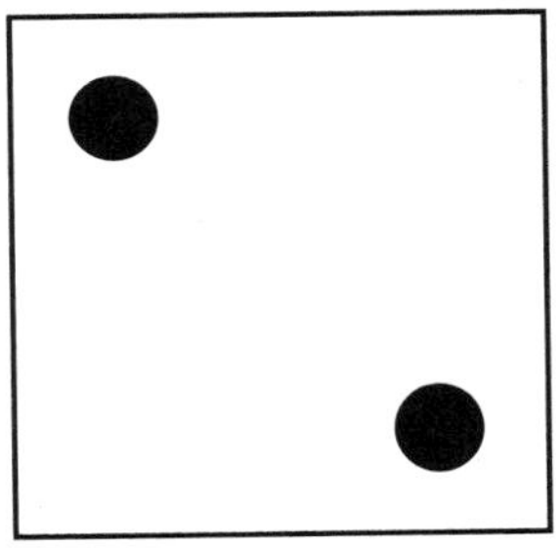

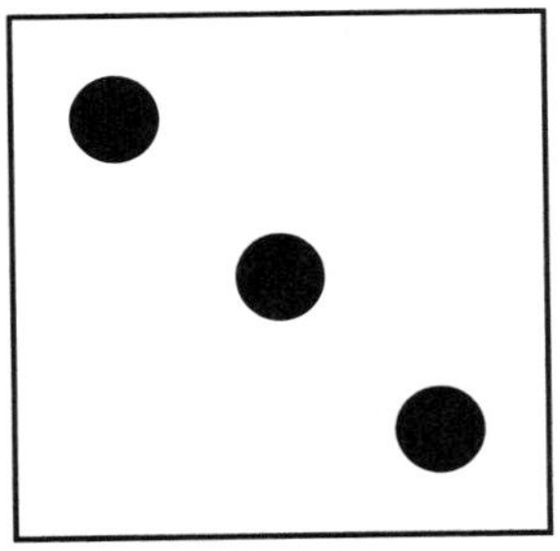

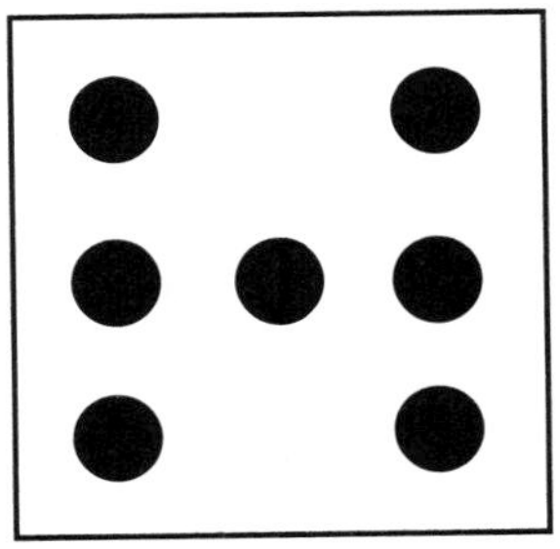

Children write the corresponding numeral beside each domino. Next, they circle the domino with more dots in each of the rows.

November: Use when children are familiar with *Domino Comparing*.

X O X O

X O X O _ _

Turtle: Children complete the pattern. **Frog:** Children circle the shortest row of clips and put an X on the longest row of clips. **Fish:** Children record the number of sides for each shape. **Spot Check:** Children color the heart red. Then they color the object **before** the heart yellow and the object **after** the heart blue.

Spot Check

Writing 10–15

0 0

1 1

2 2

3 3

4 4

5 5

Children trace the two numbers at the beginning of each row and then write the number.

December: Use when children are familiar with the *Daily Depositor*.

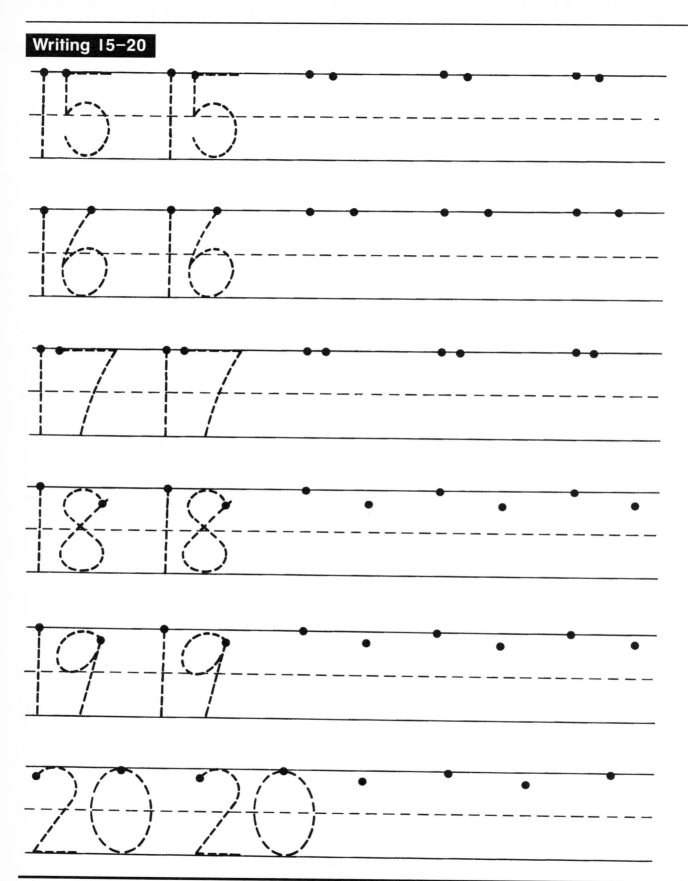

Children trace the two numbers at the beginning of each row and then write the number.

Name _____

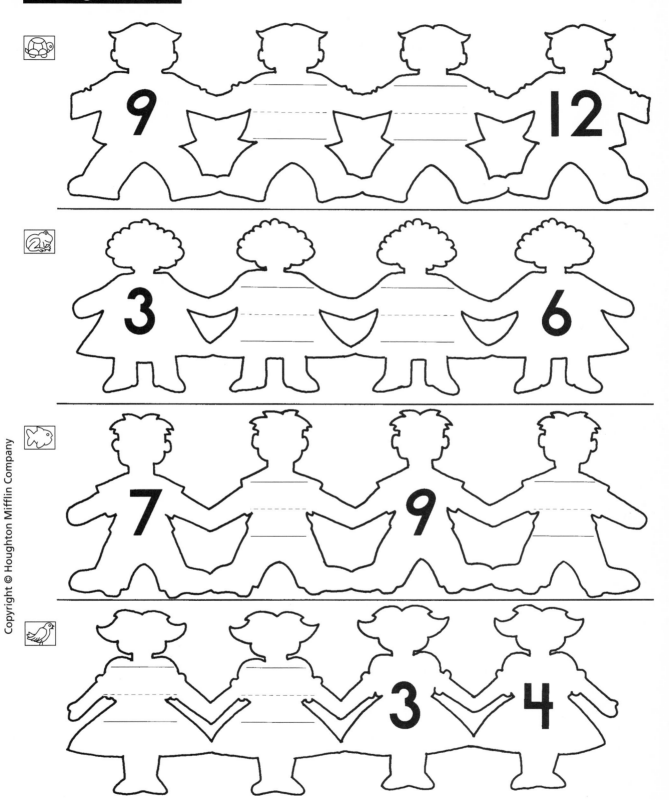

Children write the missing numbers.

December: Use when children are familiar with the *Daily Depositor*.

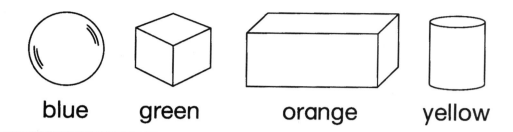

blue   green   orange   yellow

Have children color the key at the top of the page. Then children color the shapes in the picture that match.

Name _____

Length

Turtle: Children place connecting cubes on picture to form cube ruler. **Frog, Fish, and Bird:** Children measure object and write the number of cubes. **Squirrel:** Children draw an X on the ribbon they think measures 2 cubes.

December: Use when children are familiar with *Estimate the Length*.

51

How many 🖇 ?	Guess	Check

Children guess how many paper clips each object measures. They record their guesses. Then they use paper clips to check each measurement, and they record the measurement.

Name _____

Creating Patterns

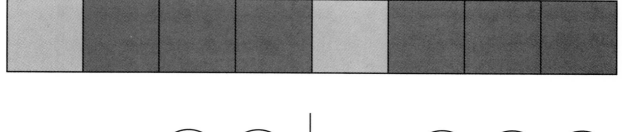

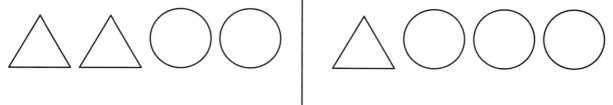

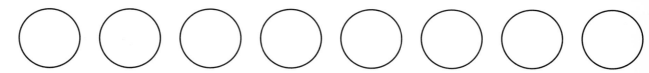

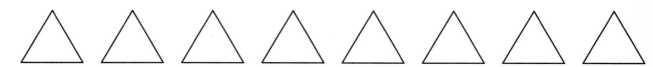

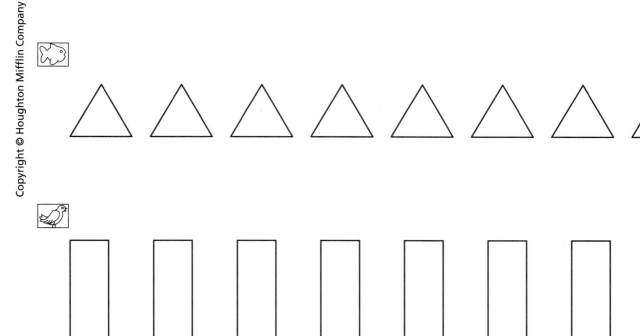

Turtle: Children circle the group that shows the same pattern as the shaded-square pattern above.
Frog: Children color circles to create a pattern. **Fish and Bird:** Children repeat the pattern they created.

December: Use when children are familiar with *Make Your Own Patterns*.

Heavier, Lighter

 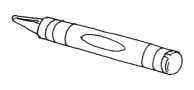 

 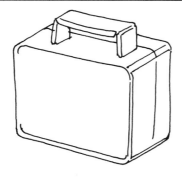 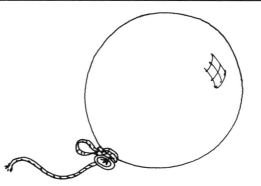

In each row, children color the **heavier** object brown.

Name _____

Lightest to Heaviest

Children cut out the pictures of the light and heavy animals and paste them in the rows above so that each row shows similar kinds of animals from **lightest** to **heaviest.**

December: Use when children are familiar with *Which Is Heavier?*

Numbers to 20

1	2	3	4	5
6	7	8	9	10
11	12	13	14	15
16	17	18	19	20

This is a class activity. Roll a number cube. Children place the corresponding number of counters on the chart, counting numbers as they cover them. Continue until the number 20 is covered.

December: Use when children are familiar with *Collect 20*.

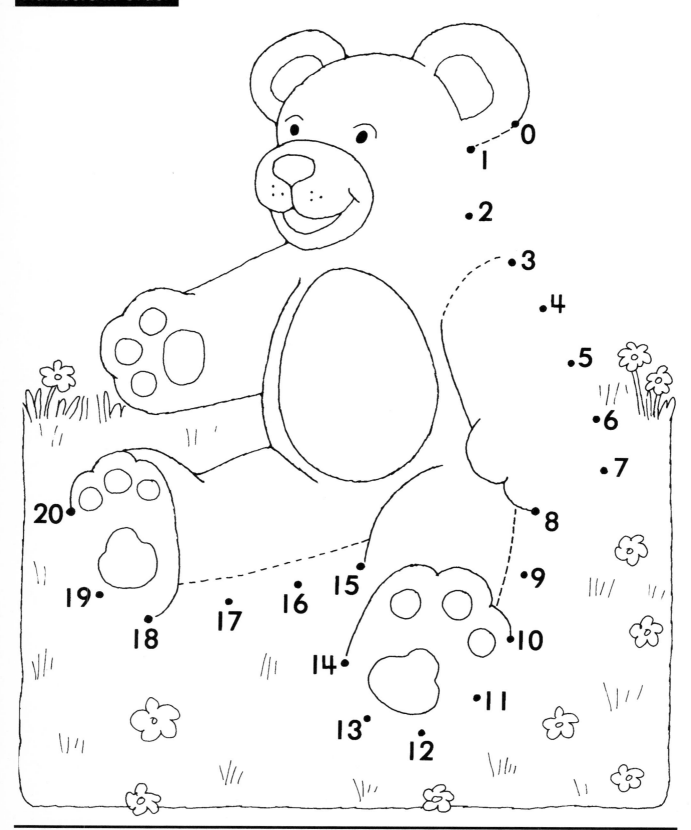

Children follow the numbers to connect the dots in order.

Name

Favorite Drink

 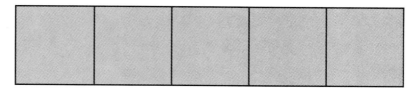

 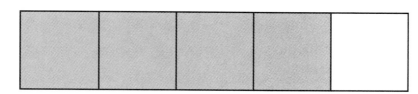

Favorite Activity

 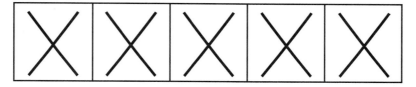

Our Pets

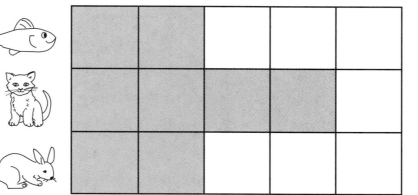

Children circle the item to indicate what the graph shows. **Turtle:** Do more children like milk or juice? **Frog:** Do more children like to paint or play with blocks? **Fish:** Which two pets do the same number of children have?

December: Use when children are familiar with *Classroom Project.*

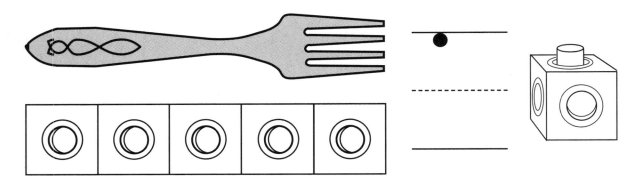

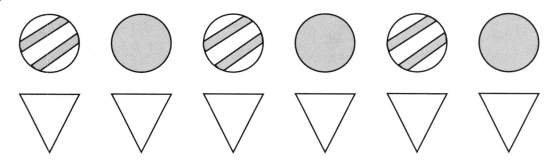

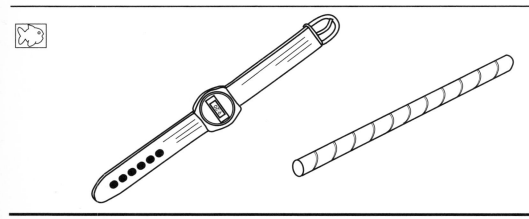

Turtle: Children measure the fork using the cube ruler shown and write the measure. **Frog:** Children color the triangles to match the AB pattern shown by the circles. **Fish:** Children draw an X on the heavier object.

Name _____

Top, Middle, and Bottom

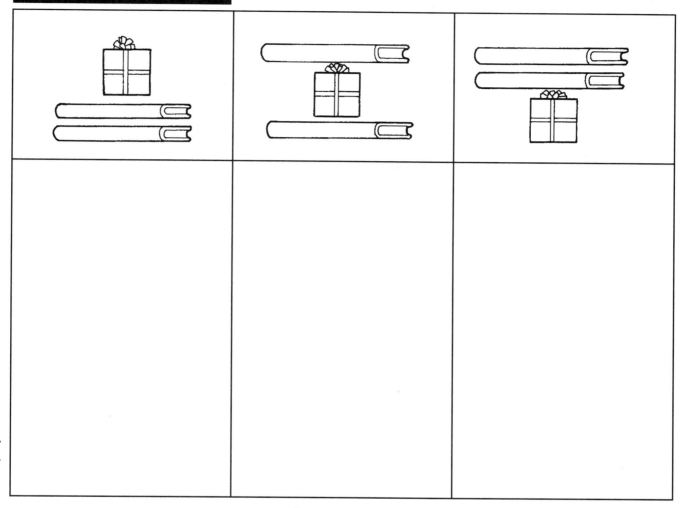

Children cut out pictures of gift boxes in the same position among other objects and paste each in the column for **top, middle,** or **bottom.**

January: Use when children are familiar with *Building Blocks of Geometry.*

Name _____

O 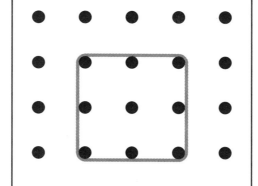 X

O 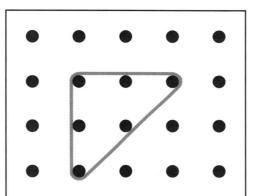 X

O 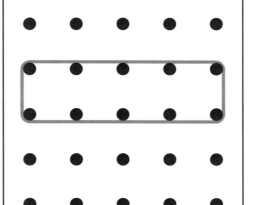 X

In each row, children count the number of **sides** and write the numeral in the space under the O. Then they count the **corners** and write the numeral in the space under the X.

January: Use when children are familiar with *Make Your Own Creations.*

Make a Design

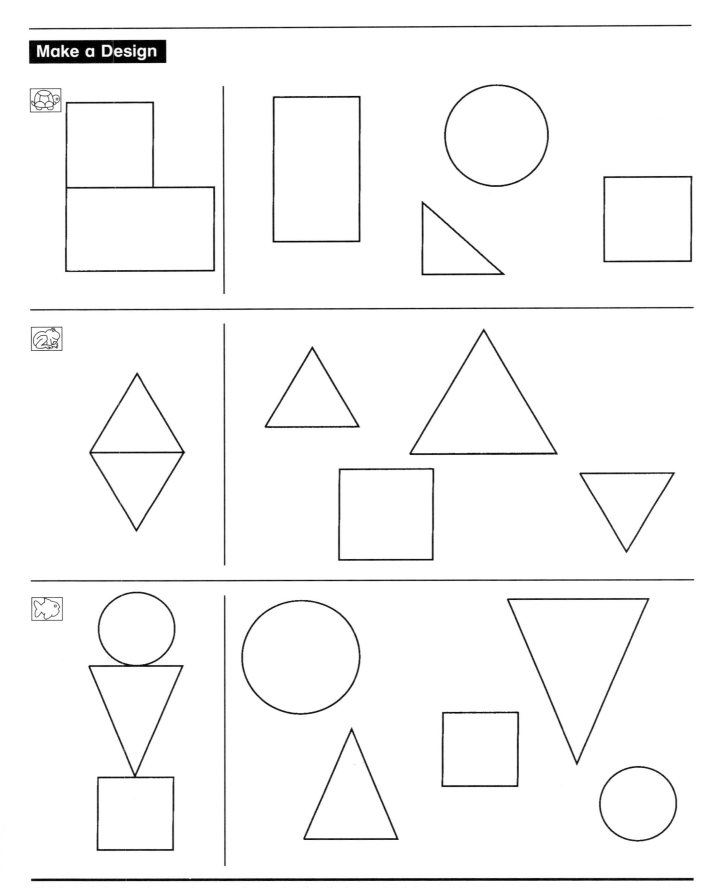

Children circle the shapes they need to make the design at the left in each row.

Name _____

How Many in All?

              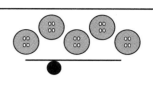

_____   _____   _____

● - - - - - - - - - -   ● - - - - - - - - - -   - - - - - - - - - -

_____   _____   _____

   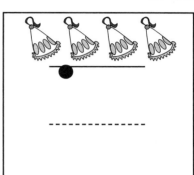

_____   _____   _____

 ● - - - - - - - - - -   ● - - - - - - - - - -   - - - - - - - - - -

_____   _____   _____

          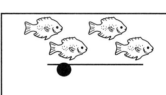

_____   _____   _____

 ● - - - - - - - - - -   ● - - - - - - - - - -   - - - - - - - - - -

_____   _____   _____

In each row, children count the number of objects in each of the first two groups and write the corresponding numerals. Then they count and write the numeral showing how many in all.

January: Use when children are familiar with *Apple Basket*.

65

Act Out Sums

$$2 + 1 = \boxed{}$$

$$2 + 3 = \boxed{}$$

$$1 + 4 = \boxed{}$$

$$4 + 2 = \boxed{}$$

Children cut out the pumpkins. They use the cutouts to tell and act out each number story. Then children write how many in all.

66 January: Use when children are familiar with *Apple Basket*.

Name _____

What Should We Wear?

In each row, children look at the picture and circle the clothing most appropriate to the season.

January: Use when children are familiar with *Weather Pictures*.

Which Holds More?

Children compare the size of the containers in each pair. Then they circle the container that can hold more.

Name _____

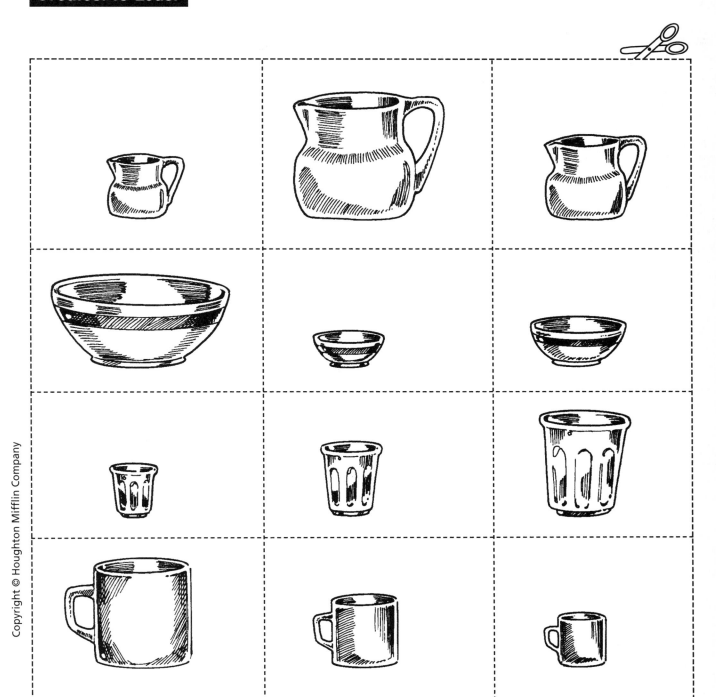

Children cut out each row of containers, order the containers from which holds **most** to which holds **least,** and paste them on paper.

January: Use when children are familiar with *Which Holds More?*

Name _____

Count and Write

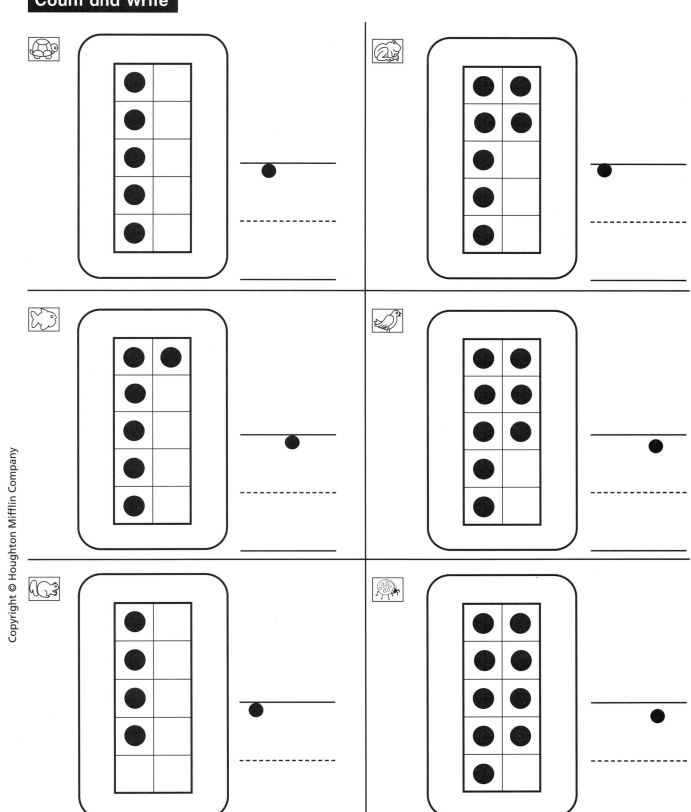

In each row, children count the dots on each card and write how many.

January: Use when children are familiar with *Ten Grid Number Matchup.*

Tens and More

🐦🐦🐦🐦🐦🐦🐦🐦🐦🐦 10
🐦🐦🐦🐦🐦🐦🐦🐦🐦🐦 20
🐦🐦🐦

23
18

🧢🧢🧢🧢🧢🧢🧢🧢🧢🧢 10
🧢🧢🧢🧢🧢🧢🧢🧢🧢🧢 20
🧢🧢🧢🧢🧢🧢🧢🧢🧢🧢 30
🧢🧢🧢🧢🧢🧢

26
36

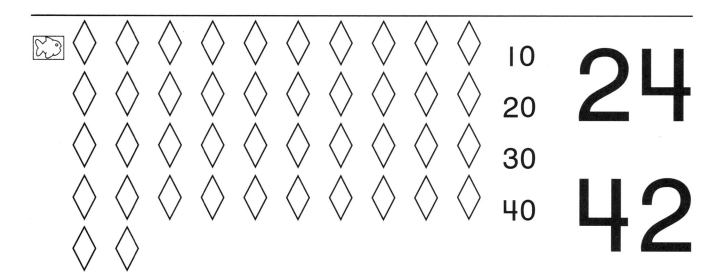

10
20
30
40

24
42

Children count the objects and then circle the number that shows how many in all.

Name _____

Writing Numbers to 30

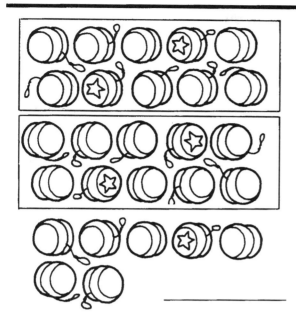

_ _ _ _ _ _ _ _ _

_____

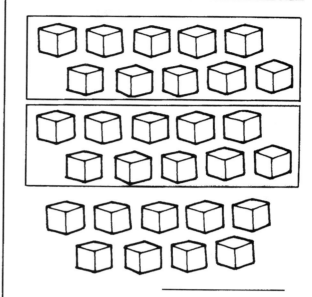

_ _ _ _ _ _ _ _ _

_____

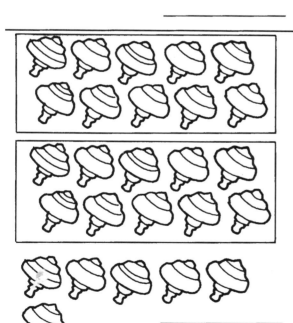

_ _ _ _ _ _ _ _ _

_____

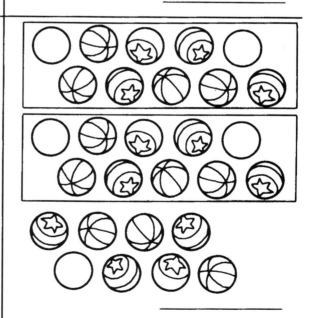

_ _ _ _ _ _ _ _ _

_____

Children count the objects and then write the number that shows how many in all.

January: Use when children are familiar with *Fill Up to 50!*

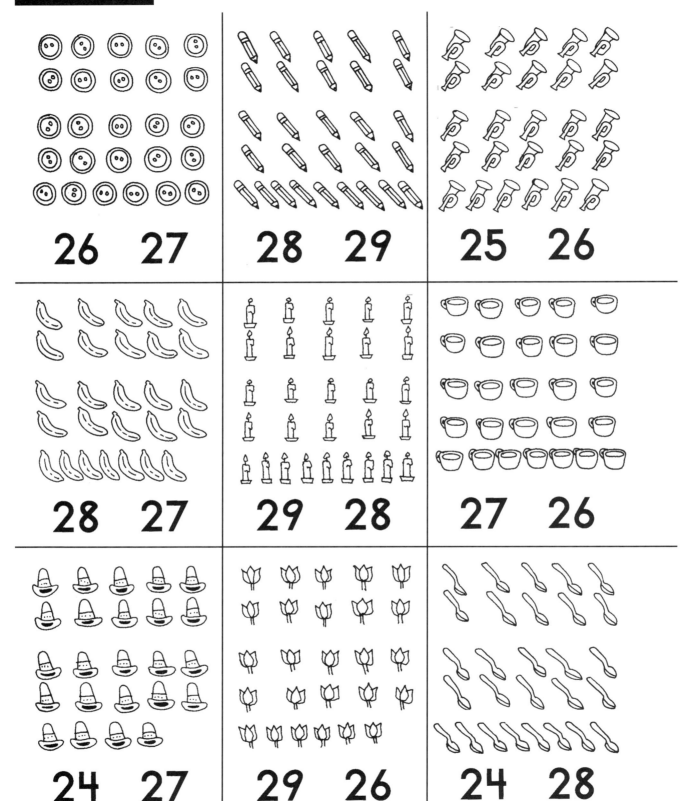

In each box, children circle groups of 10, count the objects, and circle the number that shows how many in all.

Name _____

In each row, children color in the dots and then write the numeral.

January: Use when children are familiar with *Classroom Project*.

O

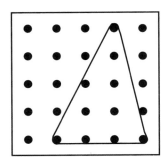

X

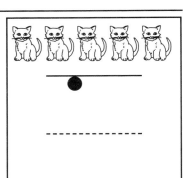

10
20

25

52

Spot Check

Turtle: Children write the number of **sides** under the O. Then they write the number of **corners** under the X.
Frog: Children write the number in each of the first two groups and then write how many in all. **Fish:** Children circle the number that shows how many. **Spot Check:** Children circle the activity that takes longer.

Name _____

Children cut out the flowers and bees at the bottom and then paste them in the boxes to complete the pattern.

February: Use when children are familiar with *Make a Pattern of Pasta*.

Name _____

Weight

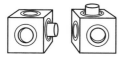 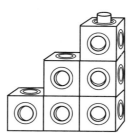 

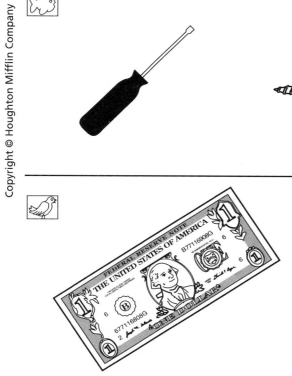  

Children circle the **heaviest** object and draw an X on the **lightest** object in each row.

February: Use when children are familiar with *How Much Does It Weigh?*

79

Cylinders

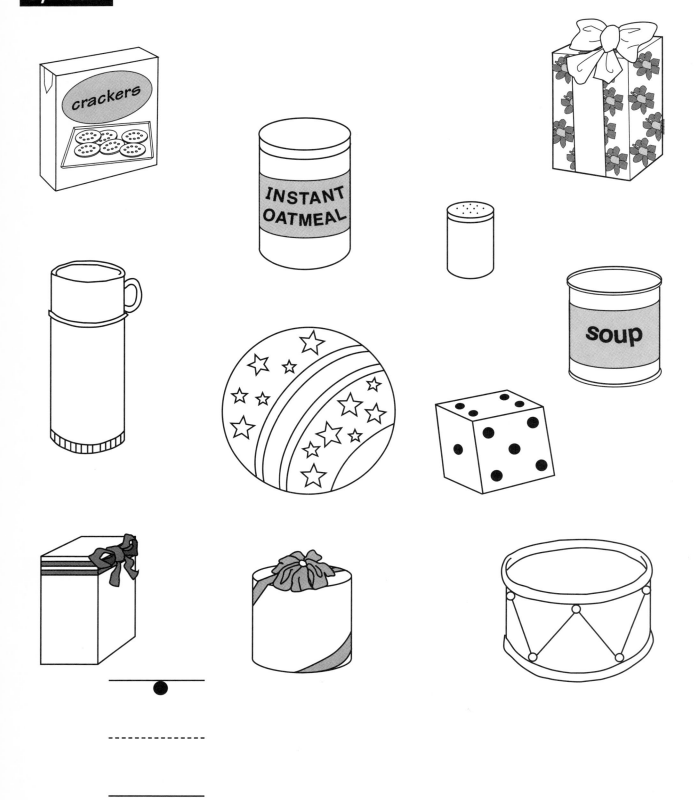

Children color the cylinders above the answer space. Then they count the cylinders and write the number.

Name _____

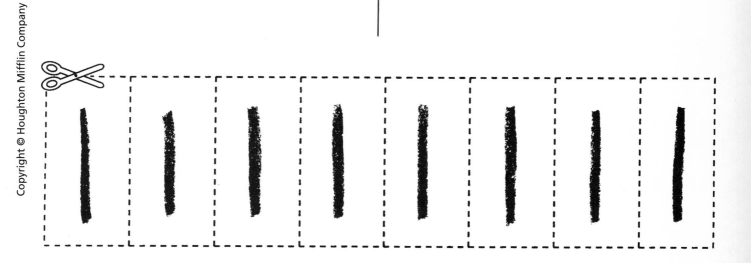

Children toss a real or play penny and record the toss by pasting a cutout tick mark in the column that matches the toss. They continue until all cutout tick marks have been used.

February: Use when children are familiar with *Guess and Graph*.

At the Store

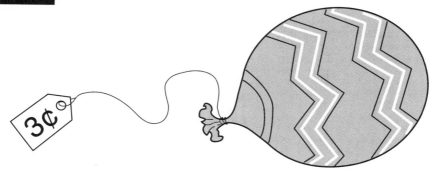

_____
•
- - - - - - -
_____ ¢

 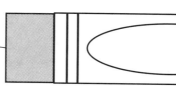

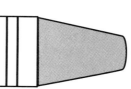

- - - - - - -
•
_____ ¢

•
- - - - - - -
¢

Children count the pennies and cross out the number equal to the price of the object. Children then count the pennies left and write the amount of change.

February: Use when children are familiar with *Break the Bank*.

2+2

Children look at what is happening in the picture story. If the number sentence matches the story, they circle the number sentence.

February: Use when children are familiar with *Break the Bank*.

How Much Is Left?

	Start with	You buy	Money left
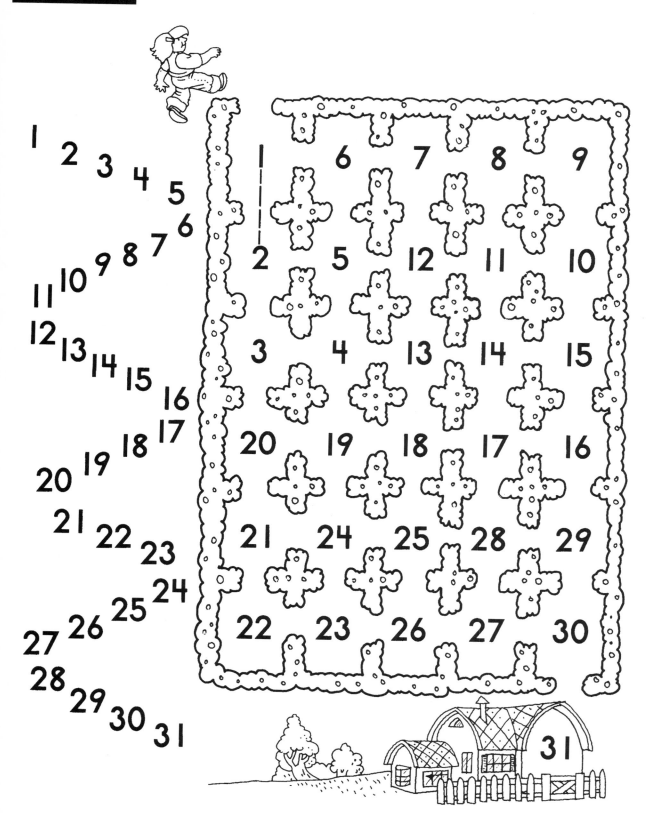	🪙🪙 🪙🪙	3¢ sharpener	_____ ¢

Number Path

1 2 3 4 5 6 7 8 9 10 11 12 13 14 15 16 17 18 19 20 21 22 23 24 25 26 27 28 29 30 31

Children connect the numbers in the maze in order to show the path to the house.

How Long?

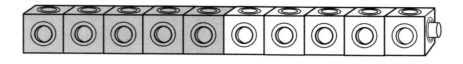

9   10   11

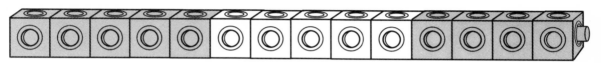

13   12   14

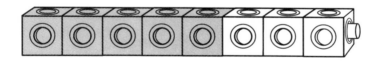

8   9   7

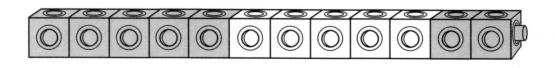

13   12   14

Children count the cubes and then circle the corresponding numeral to show how many. Then they circle the **shortest** cube train and put an X on the **longest** cube train.

February: Use when children are familiar with *Race to 31.*

1	2	3	4	5	6	7	8	9	10
11	12	13	14	15	16	17	18	19	20
21	22	23	24	25	26	27	28	29	30
31	32	33	34	35	36	37	38	39	40
41	42	43	44	45	46	47	48	49	50
51	52	53	54	55	56	57	58	59	60
61	62	63	64	65	66	67	68	69	70
71	72	73	74	75	76	77	78	79	80
81	82	83	84	85	86	87	88	89	90
91	92	93	94	95	96	97	98	99	100

Whole Class: Children count by multiples of 10 to 100, placing a counter on each number. Children then find and color red the squares with the numbers 32, 33, 37, 38, 41, 44, 46, 49, 51, 55, 59, 62, 68, 73, 77, 84, 86, and 95.

Count and Write

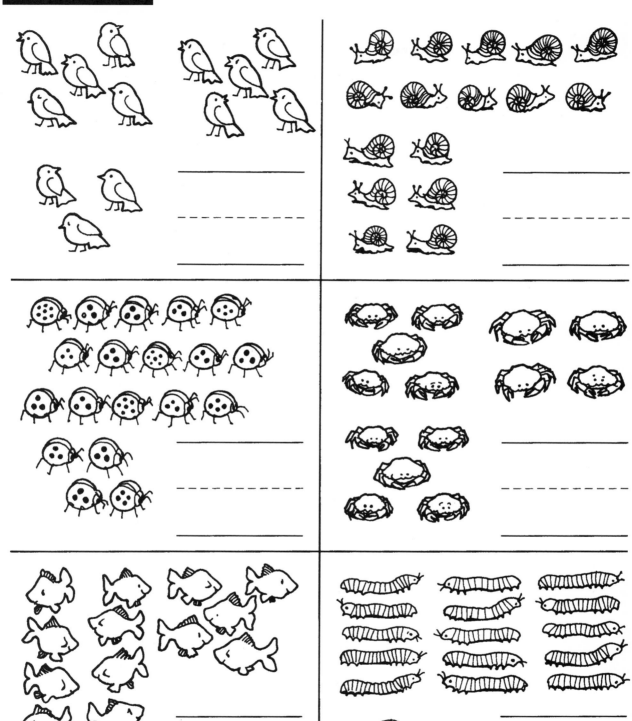

In each box, children circle groups of 5. Then they write how many in all.

February: Use when children are familiar with *Literature Corner*.

4¢

¢

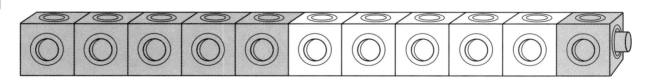

12   10   11

Turtle: Children circle the cylinder. **Frog:** Children cross out the number of pennies representing the price and then write the change. **Fish:** Children count the cubes and circle the corresponding numeral.

Counting On

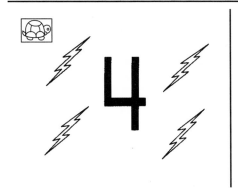 

 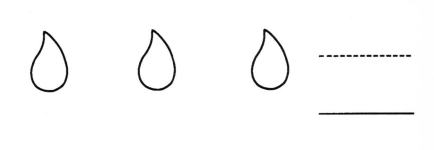

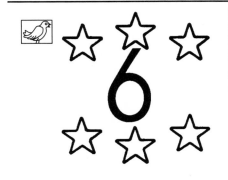 

Children count on from the number in the first box to find how many objects are in each row. Then they write the number to show how many objects there are.

March: Use when children are familiar with the *Daily Domino*.

5

6

7

8

9

In each row, children draw one more raindrop than the number shows. Then they write the number that shows one more.

Name _____

Pennies

      = 5¢

    _____ _____ ¢   _____ _____ ¢

    _____ _____ ¢   _____ _____ ¢

   _____ _____ ¢      _____ _____ ¢

   _____ _____ ¢    _____ _____ ¢

In each row, children write the numbers to show the amounts. Then they circle the greater amount in each row.

March: Use when children are familiar with the *Graph*.

93

Box It!

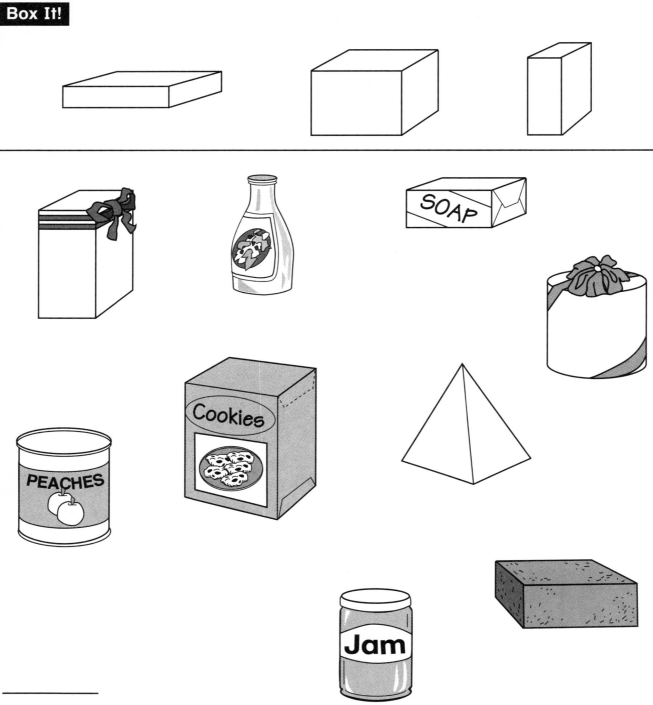

_____

- - - - - - - - - - - - - -

_____

Children circle each object that is a rectangular solid, using the examples at the top of the page for reference.
Then they count and write the total number of rectangular solids.

Name _____

○ ○ ○ ○ ○

○ ○ ○ ○ ○

○ ○ ○ ○ ○

○ ○ ○ ○ ○

○ ○ ○ ○ ○

_____   _____

- - - - - - - - - -   - - - - - - - - - -

_____ red ○   _____ white ○

Place 25 counters in a container. Children shake and carefully spill the counters. Each child records the spill by coloring the number of red counters and putting an X on the number of white counters. Then children write the results. Have children share their results.

March: Use when children are familiar with *Grab a Handful!*

Guess How Many

	Guess	Check
	2	2
	8	8
	16	16
	2	2
	12	12
	20	20
	3	3
	13	13
	18	18

Children look quickly at the jar in each row. They guess how many objects are in the jar, circle their guess, and then count and color the objects. Then they circle the actual number in the Check column.

Groups of 10

18   19   20   **18   19   20**

19   20   21   **17   18   19**

Children circle groups of 10 for each picture. Then they circle the number that shows how many objects are in that group.

March: Use when children are familiar with *Counting Tens and Ones.*

Circle Tens

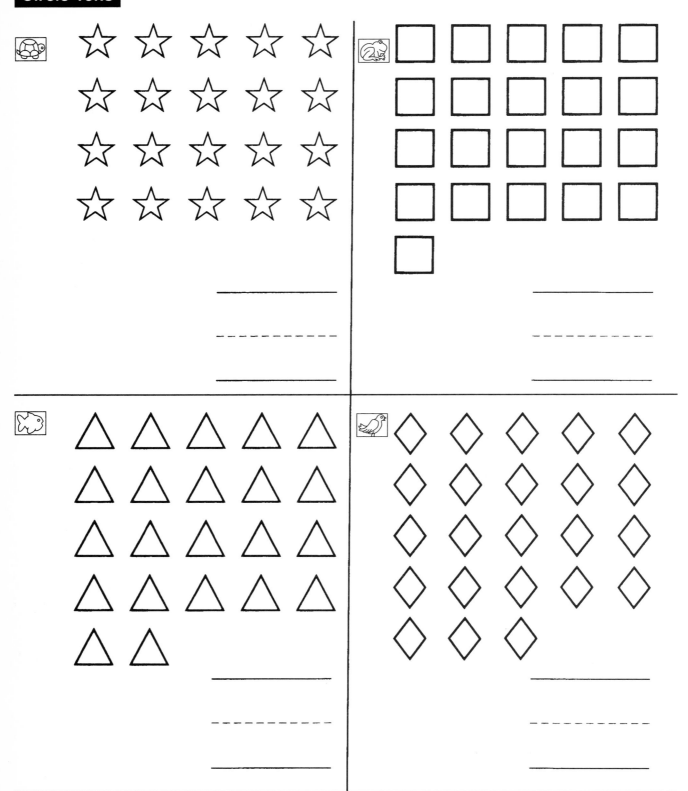

Children circle groups of 10 for each picture. Then they write the number that shows how many objects are in that group.

Name _____

Fill It Up Faster, Slower

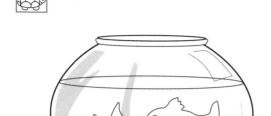

Turtle and Frog: Children circle the object they would use to fill the container at left if they wanted to fill it more quickly. **Fish:** Children circle the object they would use to fill the container more slowly.

March: Use when children are familiar with *How Much Does It Hold?*

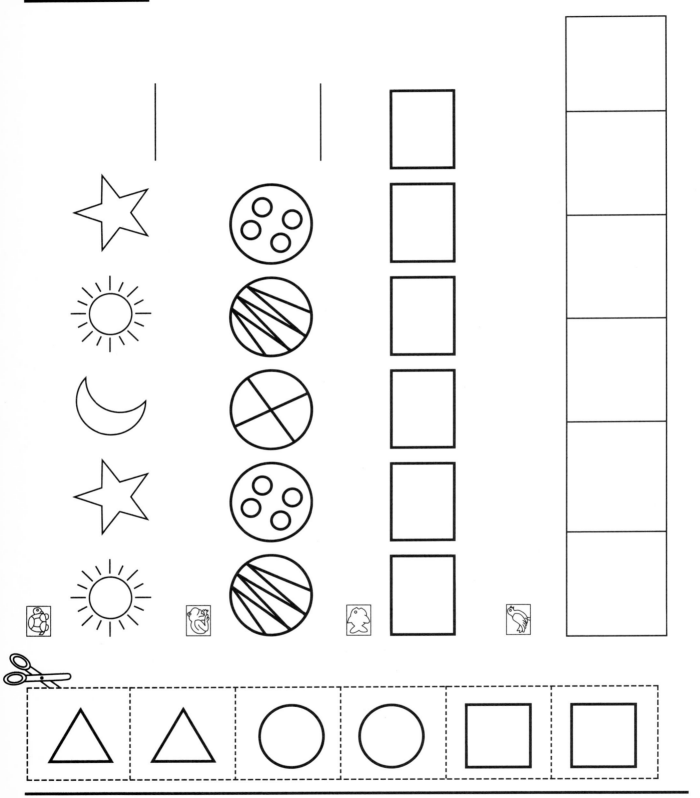

Have children turn the page so the turtle row is on top. **Turtle and Frog:** Children draw the next picture to complete the pattern. **Fish:** Children use three colors of crayons to create an ABC pattern. **Bird:** Children cut and paste the shapes to make an ABC pattern.

Name _____

Count and Compare

_____

- - - - - - - - - - -

_____ more

_____

- - - - - - - - - - -

_____ more

_____

- - - - - - - - - - -

_____ more

_____

- - - - - - - - - - -

_____ more

In each row, children determine which has more by drawing lines to show one-to-one correspondence. Children write the numeral showing how many more and draw a picture showing the correct object.

March: Use when children are familiar with *The Penny Tosser*.

Whole to Parts

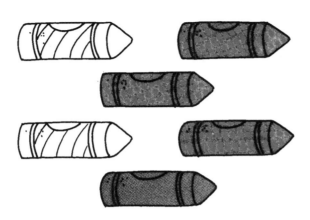

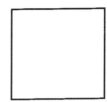

  and

---

 and

For each group, children write how many are in the whole set. Then they write how many are in each part.

Name _____

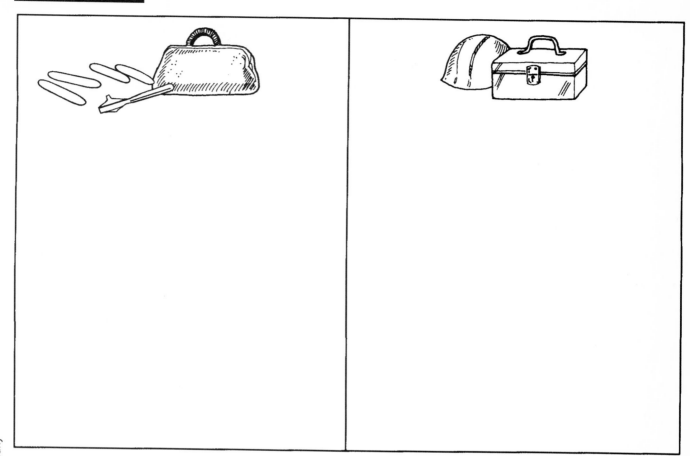

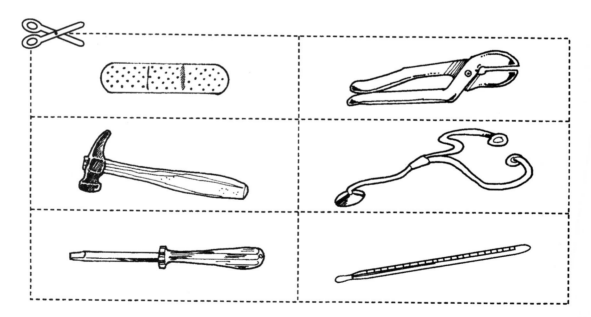

Children cut and paste the tools used by a doctor below the bag and the tools used by a carpenter below the toolbox.

March: Use when children are familiar with *Classroom Project.*

103

Name _____

Add the Counters

 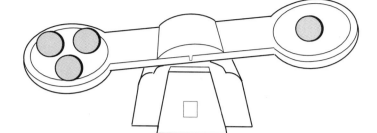 

 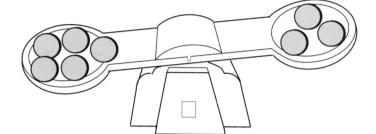 

 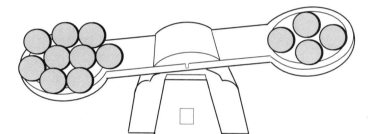 

 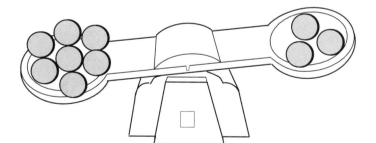 

 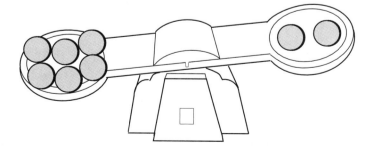 

In each row, children circle the number of counters it will take to balance the scale.

March: Use when children are familiar with *Domino Fill Up.*

_____

_____ ¢

_____

_____ ¢

_____

_____ more

_____ _____ _____ _____

Spot Check

Turtle: Children write the amounts and then circle the greater amount. **Frog:** Children draw lines to show one-to-one correspondence. Then they write the numeral showing how many more and draw the correct shape. **Fish:** Children circle the number of counters it will take to balance the scale. **Spot Check:** Children repeat the AABB pattern.

Name _____

Money in the Bank

 12¢    7¢

 11¢    6¢

 15¢    20¢

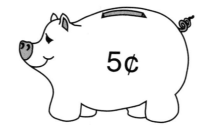 5¢    20¢

Children count the coins and then circle the piggy bank that shows that amount.

April: Use when children are familiar with the *Daily Depositor.*

Equal Parts

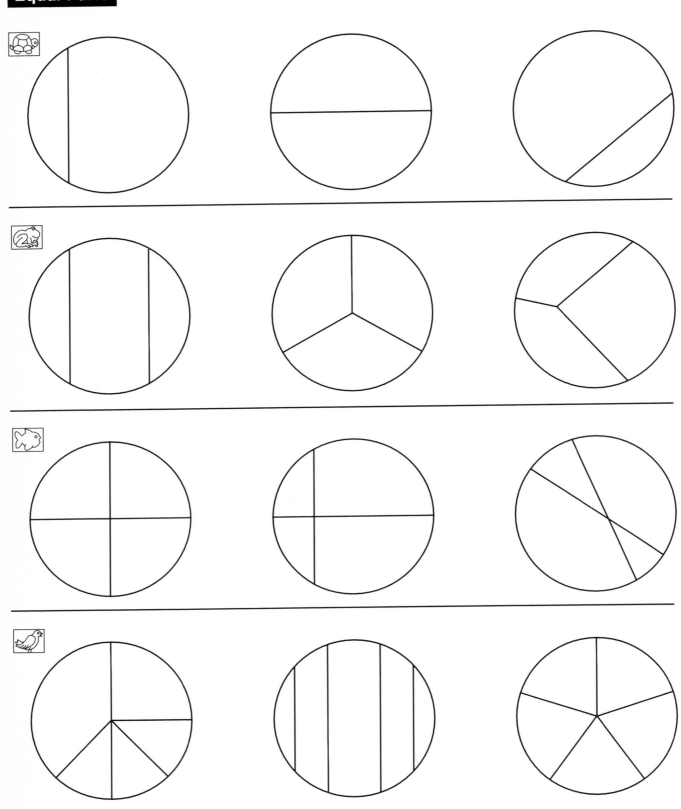

In each row, children color the circle that shows equal parts.

Shapes in Half

Children draw a line to divide each shape in half.

April: Use when children are familiar with *Fractional Play*.

How Many Cubes?

red						
blue						
green						

_____

-------------- 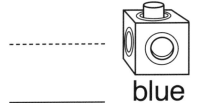 red

_____

--------------  blue

_____

_____

-------------- green

_____

Working in pairs or small groups, children color cubes on the page according to the labels. They place a red cube, a blue cube, and a green cube in a paper bag. Without looking, one child pulls out a cube. Each child records the color of the cube on his or her graph. The cube is replaced, and the steps are repeated until one row in the graph is filled. Then children record how many cubes of each color were picked.

Name _____

How Much?

_____ _____ _____

---- ₵ + ---- ₵ = ---- ₵

_____ _____

---- ₵ + ---- ₵ = ---- ₵

_____ _____ _____

---- ₵ + ---- ₵ = ---- ₵

Children place pennies where they are shown in each row. They count the pennies in each group and write each amount. Then they combine the two groups of pennies, count, and write the total amount.

April: Use when children are familiar with *Money Math Stories*.

111

Subtract Money

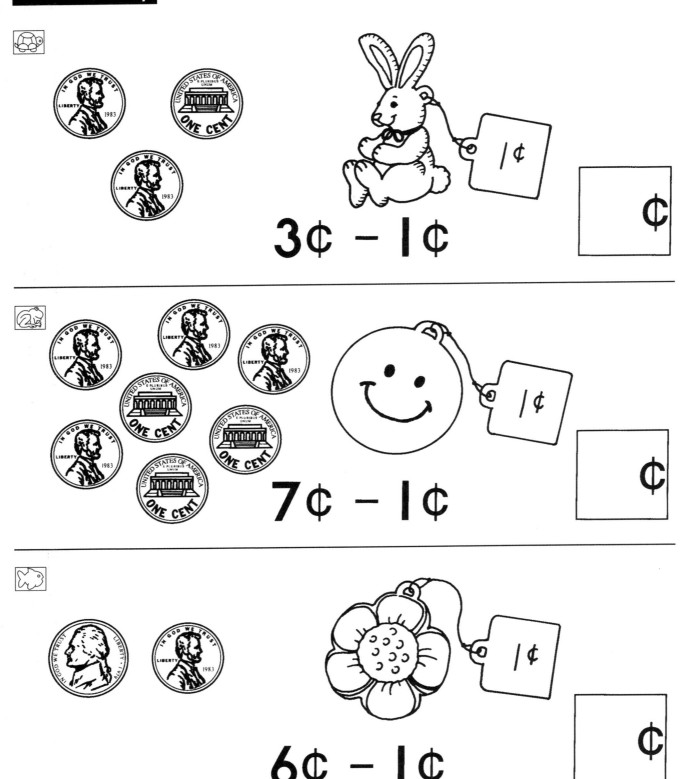

$$3¢ - 1¢$$

$$7¢ - 1¢$$

$$6¢ - 1¢$$

In each row, children use pennies and nickels to show how much money they start with. They move coins to show how much they spend. Then they cross out the same coins and write how much money is left.

Name _____

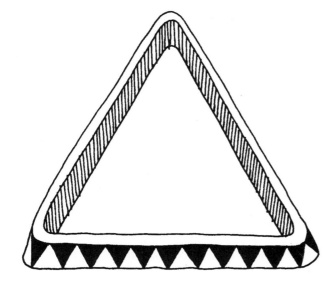
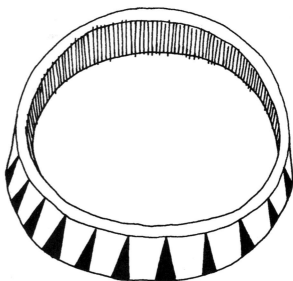

△ + ◯ = ☐ | △ + ◯ = ☐

△ + ◯ = ☐ | △ + ◯ = ☐

△ + ◯ = ☐ | △ + ◯ = ☐

Children cut out the elephants. They put some in the triangle and some in the circle. Then they record the numbers in a triangle and a circle below and write the sum in the box. They continue until all the boxes are filled.

April: Use when children are familiar with *Addition and Subtraction Stories.*

Open and Closed Shapes

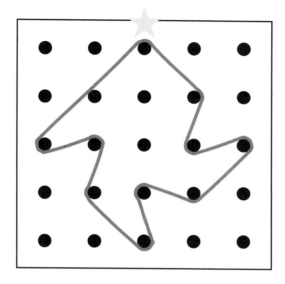
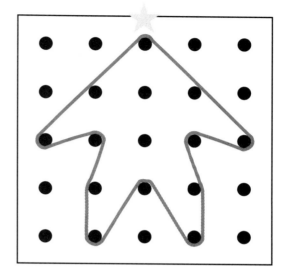

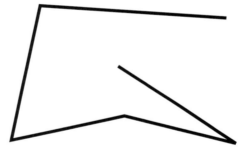

Turtle: Children circle the geoboard that shows a shape made with the geoband touching 12 pegs. Children may want to use the star as a guide to start and stop counting. **Frog:** Children circle each closed shape.

April: Use when children are familiar with *Geoboard Follow the Leader*.

How Long?

In each row, children circle the activity that takes the most time and draw an X on the activity that takes the least time. **Turtle:** filling a pool, a glass, or a sink; **Frog:** frog jumping from one lily pad to the next, squirrel eating acorn, or bird building nest; **Fish:** hanging up jacket, washing clothes, or laying out clothes.

April: Use when children are familiar with *How Much Time?*

Name _____

Calculator Counting

$$19$$

_____

- - - - - - - - - - - - - - - -

_____

$$21$$

_____

- - - - - - - - - - - - - - - -

_____

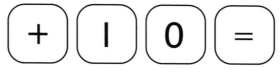

$$4 \quad + \quad 1 \quad 0 \quad =$$

_____

- - - - - - - - - - - - - - - -

_____

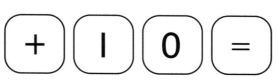

$$14 \quad + \quad 1 \quad 0 \quad =$$

_____

- - - - - - - - - - - - - - - -

_____

Children use calculators to display the number shown in the box and then input the key sequence depicted. Then they write the answer.

April: Use when children are familiar with *Counting with a Calculator.*

How Many More?

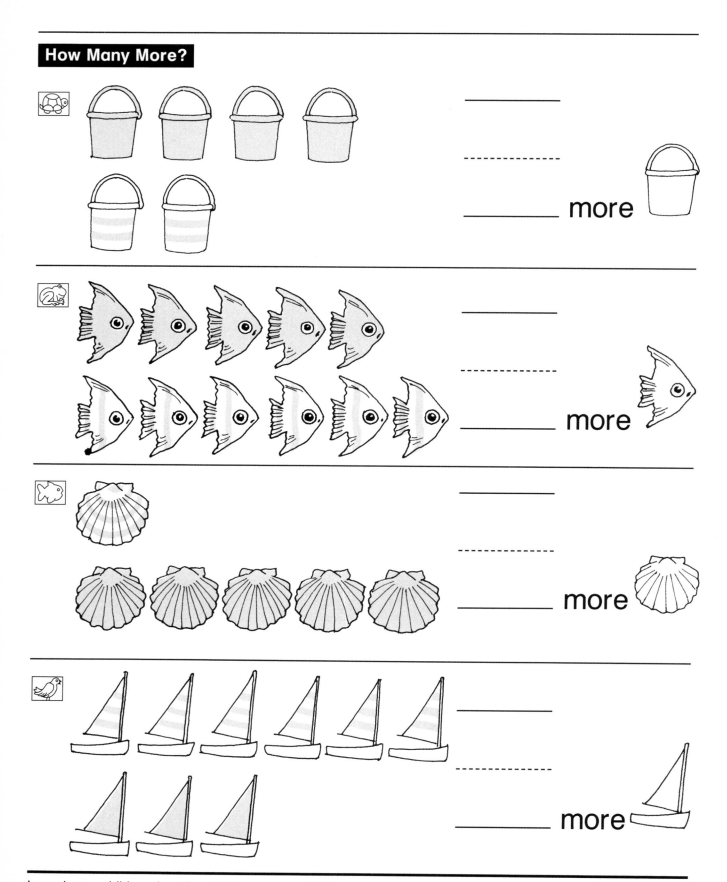

_____ more

_____ more

_____ more

_____ more

In each row, children draw lines between rows of objects to show one-to-one correspondence. Then they write the numeral to show how many more and color or draw stripes on the rebus to show which kind has more.

Name _____

Trading Pennies

_____   _____   _____

    ¢

_____   _____   _____

_____   _____   _____

    ¢

_____   _____   _____

In each row, children circle groups of 5 pennies. They write the number of nickels they could trade for and the number of pennies left over. Then they write how much in all.

April: Use when children are familiar with *5! 10! 15! 20!*

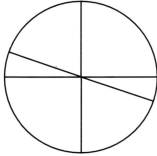 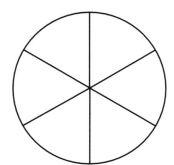 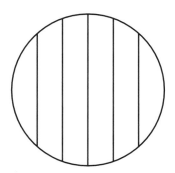

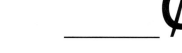 

_____ ¢ + _____ ¢ = _____ ¢

_____

- - - - - - - -

_____ more

Turtle: Children color the circle that is divided into 6 equal parts. **Frog:** Children count the pennies and then write each amount and the total. **Fish:** Children draw lines to show one-to-one correspondence, write how many more, and then show which kind has more.

Money Sums

$$2¢ \ + \ 1¢ \ = \ \boxed{¢}$$

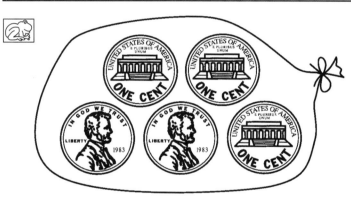

$$5¢ \ + \ 1¢ \ = \ \boxed{¢}$$

 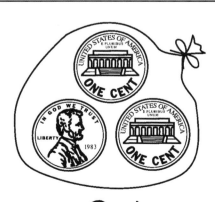

$$3¢ \ + \ 1¢ \ = \ \boxed{¢}$$

Children write the sum of the money in the bag and the money being added.

May/June: Use when children are familiar with *Acting Out Number Stories.*

Counting Back

4 − 1 = __

3 − 1 = __

5 − 1 = __

Children tell a number story about each picture. Then they count back 1 and write the difference.

Name _____

+ or −

2 ☐ 1

7 ☐ 2

6 ☐ 2

Children cut out the pictures and paste them where they belong. Then they write + or − in the box.

May/June: Use when children are familiar with *Acting Out Number Stories.*

123

The Sum Is Five

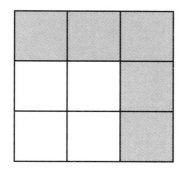

_____   _____
- - - - - - - - + - - - - - - - = **5**
_____   _____

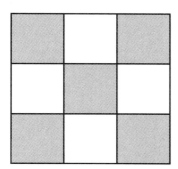

_____   _____
- - - - - - - - + - - - - - - - = **5**
_____   _____

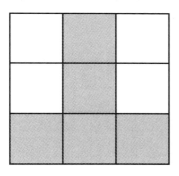

_____   _____
- - - - - - - - + - - - - - - - = **5**
_____   _____

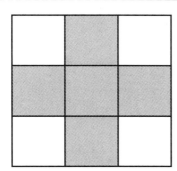

_____   _____
- - - - - - - - + - - - - - - - = **5**
_____   _____

In each row, children look at the shading on the 3 x 3 grid. Then they record a different combination to go with each arrangement of 5 shaded squares.

May/June: Use when children are familiar with *Exploring Number Shapes*.

Calculate and Color

1	2	3	4	5	6	7	8	9	10
11	12	13	14	15	16	17	18	19	20
21	22	23	24	25	26	27	28	29	30
31	32	33	34	35	36	37	38	39	40
41	42	43	44	45	46	47	48	49	50
51	52	53	54	55	56	57	58	59	60
61	62	63	64	65	66	67	68	69	70
71	72	73	74	75	76	77	78	79	80
81	82	83	84	85	86	87	88	89	90
91	92	93	94	95	96	97	98	99	100

Children input [10] on the calculator and color 10 on the chart green. Then they press [+] [10] [=] and color 20 green. Children continue to press [+] [10] [=] and color the answer green each time until they reach 100. Then they press [−] [1] [=] until they reach 91, coloring each answer yellow on the chart.

Name _____

How Many Dots?

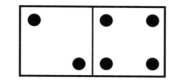

_____   _____   _____

- - - - - - - - - -   **+**   - - - - - - - - - -   **=**   - - - - - - - - - -

_____   _____   _____

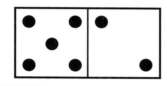

_____   _____   _____

- - - - - - - - - -   **+**   - - - - - - - - - -   **=**   - - - - - - - - - -

_____   _____   _____

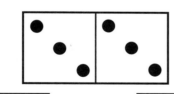

_____   _____   _____

- - - - - - - - - -   **+**   - - - - - - - - - -   **=**   - - - - - - - - - -

_____   _____   _____

In each row, children count the dots on the left domino half and then write the number. They do the same for the right half. Then they count the total number of dots and write the sum.

May/June: Use when children are familiar with *Domino Sums*.

127

Trade for Dimes and Nickels

In each row, children trade pennies for nickels and nickels for dimes. They cut and paste to show their trades. Children may use coins to help them.

May/June: Use when children are familiar with *5! 10! 15! 20! with Dimes.*

Name _____

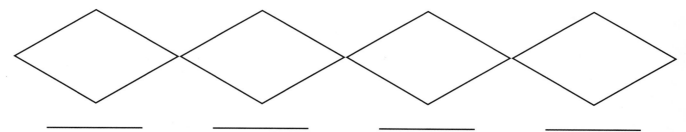

_____   _____   _____   _____

- - - - - -   - - - - - -   - - - - - -   - - - - - -

_____   _____   _____   _____

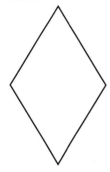 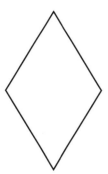 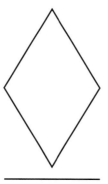 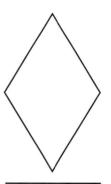 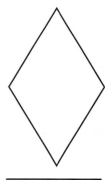

_____   _____   _____   _____   _____

- - - - -   - - - - -   - - - - -   - - - - -   - - - - -

_____   _____   _____   _____   _____

In each row, children place their triangle pattern blocks on the outlines. Removing one pattern block, they draw a line on each rhombus to show the two triangles that form the rhombus. Then they write the numbers to show counting by 2's.

May/June: Use when children are familiar with *Cover-Up.*

Making Change

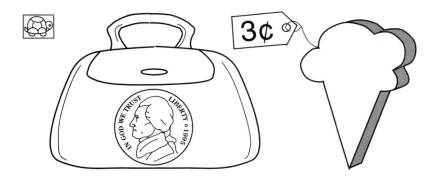

3¢

_____

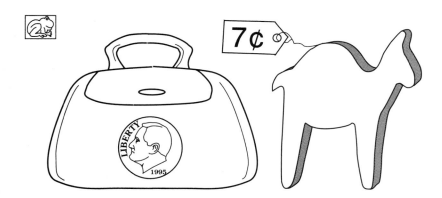

7¢

_____

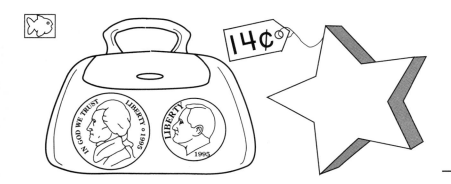

14¢

_____

All rows: Using the coins shown, children determine the change due after they buy each item. Then they cut and paste to show the correct amount of change.

Comparing Dominoes

In each row, children circle the domino with more dots. Then they write the numeral to show how many more.

May/June: Use when children are familiar with *Domino Difference*.

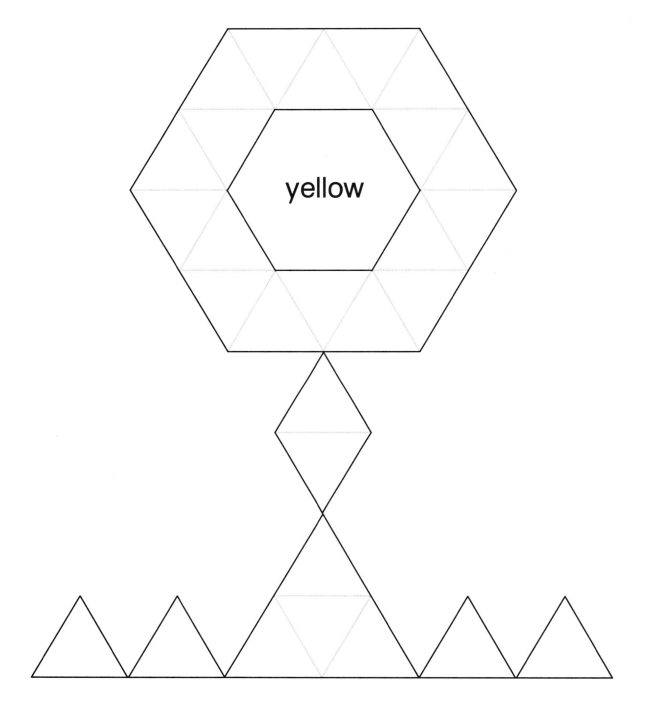

yellow

Children place a yellow pattern block on the shape where shown. They must use red, green, and blue pattern blocks to cover the rest of the picture. Children use matching-color crayons to record their complete pattern on the page. Then they share the different ways the shape was colored.

Name _____

What Can You Buy?

    13¢  16¢

    15¢  20¢

     40¢ 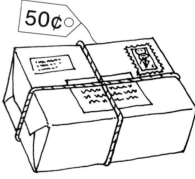 50¢

   12¢  14¢

In each row, children circle the item that they can buy or mail with the money shown.

May/June: Use when children are familiar with *Classroom Project*.

133

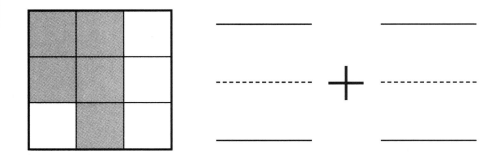

$$\underline{\qquad} + \underline{\qquad} = 5$$

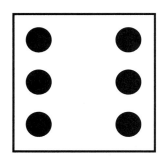 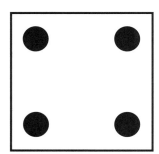

$$\underline{\qquad\qquad}$$

 *Spot Check*

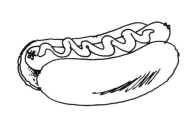

Turtle: Children look at the shading on the grid and write a number sentence with a sum of 5. **Frog:** Children circle the domino that has more dots. Then they write the numeral to show how many more. **Fish:** Children circle the item that they can buy with the coins shown. **Spot Check:** Children circle the food that takes the most time to eat and draw an X on the food that takes the least time to eat.

Numeral Writing

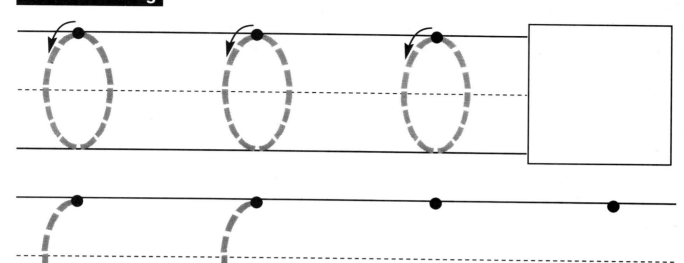

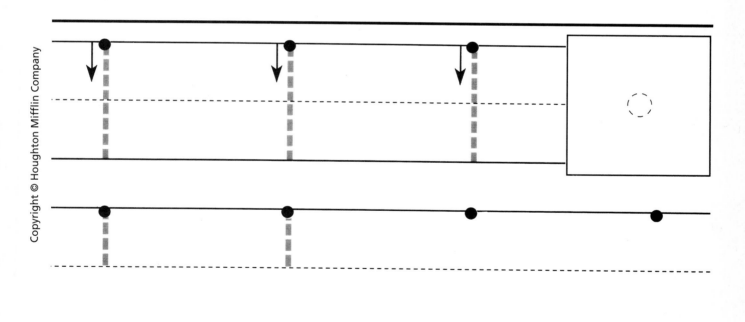

Children color in the dot in the domino half and write the numbers.

Numeral Writing

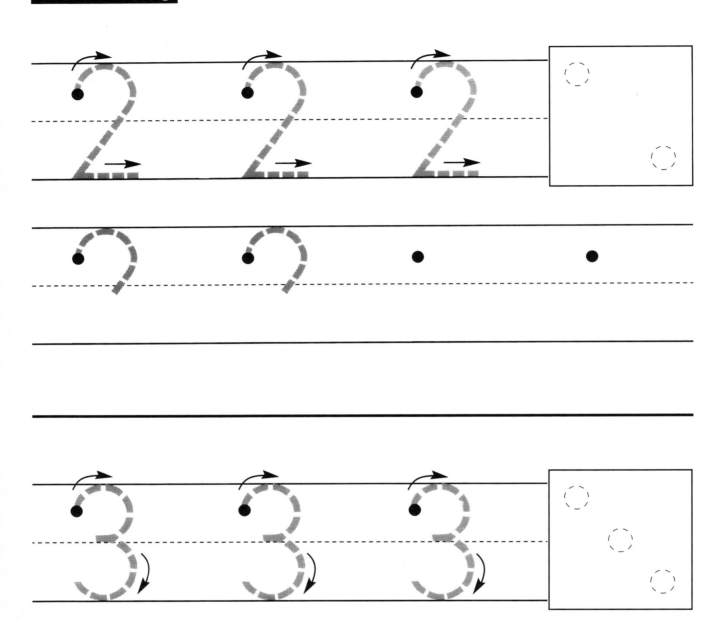

Children color in the dots in the domino halves and write the numbers.

Numeral Writing

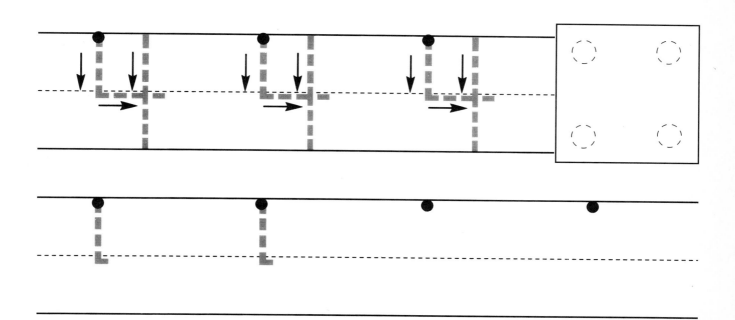

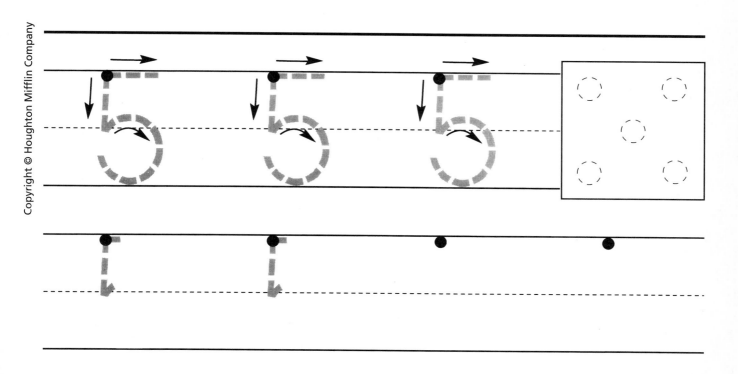

Children color in the dots in the domino halves and write the numbers.

Numeral Writing

Numeral Writing

Children color in the dots in the domino halves and write the numbers.

Copyright © Houghton Mifflin Company

Name _____

Numeral Writing

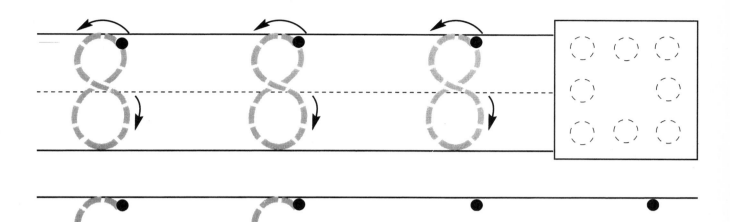

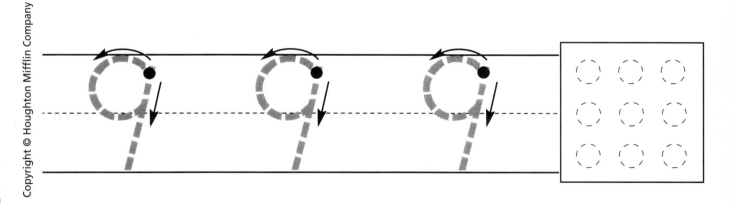

Children color in the dots in the domino halves and write the numbers.

Numeral Writing